BE YOUR OWN LITERARY AGENT

BE YOUR OWN LITERARY AGENT

The Ultimate Insider's Guide to Getting Published

MARTIN P. LEVIN

1◐ TEN SPEED PRESS
BERKELEY, CALIFORNIA

A Kirsty Melville book

The author and publisher would like to thank the following for permission to use previously published material: Gerald Gunther, author of *Learned Hand: The Man and the Judge* (Alfred A. Knopf, 1994); International Creative Management, Inc., *True Grit*, © 1969 by Charles Portis; from the book *Where Angels Walk: True Stories of Heavenly Visitors* by Joan Wester Anderson, © 1992 by Joan Wester Anderson, published by Barton & Brett, Publishers, Inc.; Penguin Books, U.S.A., Inc., from *Don Juan de Marco* by Jeremy Leven, novelization, Jean Blake White, © 1995 by New Line Productions, Inc. and Jeremy Leven, used by permission of Dutton Signet, a division of Penguin Books, U.S.A., Inc.

1☺
TEN SPEED PRESS
P.O. Box 7123
Berkeley, CA 94707

Text & cover design: Sarah Levin
Printed in the United States

Library of Congress Catalog Card Number 95-60755

ISBN 0-89815-772-2
  2   3   4   5—100   99   98   97   96

Contents

Introduction   **vii**

CHAPTER 1   Selling the First Book: Stories of
                  the Rich and Famous   **1**

CHAPTER 2   Making Your Book the Best It Can Be   **7**

CHAPTER 3   The Eight-Step Program for Selling
                  Your Book   **12**

CHAPTER 4   Finding the Best Publisher for Your Book   **20**

CHAPTER 5   What Goes on behind Closed Doors   **36**

CHAPTER 6   The Book Proposal: Where the
                  Author and Editor Meet   **45**

CHAPTER 7   Models—Query Letter, Cover Letter, Summary,
                  Table of Contents, Sample Chapter, and Bio   **53**

                  Nonfiction Query Letter   **54**

                  Fiction Query Letter   **56**

                  Nonfiction Cover Letter   **58**

                  Fiction Cover Letter   **60**

                  Nonfiction Summary   **62**

                  Nonfiction Table of Contents   **67**

                  Nonfiction Expanded Table of Contents   **69**

                  Fiction Sample Chapter   **73**

                  Nonfiction Sample Chapter   **78**

                  Resume Bio   **88**

                  Narrative Bio   **89**

                  Complete Proposal   **89**

CHAPTER 8   The Editor and the First-Time
                  Author Negotiate   **103**

CHAPTER 9   Creating Contract Literacy   **112**

CHAPTER 10   The Contract Reality Check   **135**

CHAPTER 11   Reprise   **164**

THE TOOL KIT 167

Appendixes and References

APPENDIX A   PubSpeak—The Publishing Industry's
Private Language   **168**

APPENDIX B   How to Use *Literary Market Place*
to Find Your Publisher and Editor   **179**

APPENDIX C   Best Bets—The Publishers Most Likely
to Read and Accept Your Book   **192**

APPENDIX D   Manuscript Submission Record   **205**

APPENDIX E   References   **207**

Acknowledgments   **209**

About the Author   **210**

Index   **212**

Introduction

■ How would you like help from a literary agent who would read your book before it is submitted to an editor, provide encouragement and advice to you in making changes, map out a marketing strategy for selling your book, and help you prepare an effective proposal for submission to the right editor in the right publishing house? And then, having sold your book, how would you like a publishing lawyer to help you negotiate the business terms and review the publisher's contract?

Realistically, experienced literary agents are not often available to an unpublished author. And sometimes, publishing lawyers are hard to find and expensive. The promise of this book, *Be Your Own Literary Agent*, is that you can learn to perform the functions of a literary agent, sell your book successfully, and by becoming contract literate, reduce the fee you pay for legal services.

As an experienced publisher and now a publishing lawyer, I believe you can *Be Your Own Literary Agent*. I have been involved in publishing for over four decades. For thirty-four years, as a publishing executive, I worked closely with agents and authors. I bought books on my own and later supervised editorial acquisition programs, spending over $100 million for publishing rights. I was involved in buying fiction and nonfiction, adult and juvenile, hard-cover and paperback, and popular and professional books. And for the last ten years, as an agent and publishing lawyer, I have worked with authors in developing best-selling books, negotiating their contracts, and getting the books public attention.

Before writing this book, to test its premise, I conducted a survey of editors who are currently receiving unsolicited manuscripts. They reported that when the manuscript is worthwhile and properly presented, they do acquire books from unagented authors. The rejection rate for unsolicited manuscripts is so high, they said, because most of the books they receive are not professionally written or presented.

Finally, prior to publication, I submitted this book to senior editorial executives and agents. They read what you are about to read. They added their wisdom to what I had written and agreed that if you follow the advice in this book you can *Be Your Own Literary Agent* and be successfully published.

While writing this book, I visualized you sitting in my office. I wrote in the same style I use when I talk to a client. As you read *Be Your Own Literary Agent*, imagine me at your side. (I recognize that there are two genders. I have used "her" as a pronoun for the author and editor, and "him" for the agent and publisher. I hope you will accept this and appreciate the intention to be representative of my readers.)

I will encourage you to continue, despite setbacks, to write for publication, and I'll share with you stories of how authors such as Tom Clancy, Pat Conroy, and many other rich and famous writers sold their first books without an agent (Chapter 1). I will advise you, if you are receiving rejection letters, how you can find someone to help you improve your manuscript so that you will be able to submit your best work (Chapter 2). I will share with you my "Eight-Step Program for Selling Your Book," and describe every element of this plan in detail (Chapters 3 and 4).

I will introduce you to editors who will tell you what to include in your proposal, how your submission will be judged, how soon you will hear from them, and who will provide a score of other tips to improve the odds of having your proposal read and accepted (Chapter 5). I will describe the rules for creating an effective proposal and illustrate them with over thirty pages of model query letters, cover letters, summaries, sample chapters, and bios. You will be able to compare your own work to the models and make improvements, if needed, before you submit your proposal (Chapters 6 and 7).

Assuming your success in finding a publisher, I will sit by your side as you negotiate the business terms of your contract, comparing it to what, based on my experience, is a "bad," a "fair," and a "good" deal. Then, as I do with my class in Publishing Law at New York Law School, I will help you become contract literate, explaining the copyright provisions and the legal terms you will find in a standard publisher's contract, paragraph by paragraph (Chapters 8, 9, and 10).

Along the way, there may be strange terms or unfamiliar techniques. At the back of the book is a Tool Kit which contains a glossary of terms; step-by-step instructions on how to use *Literary Market Place* (*LMP*), the agent's primary reference tool; and a list of smaller publishers who are more likely to read and buy your manuscript.

When we have completed our time together, I believe you will be able to *Be Your Own Literary Agent*. No one can promise to sell your book. No literary agent sells every book he offers. What I can promise is that you will have the information you need to *Be Your Own Literary Agent* and that the odds in favor of selling your book on your own will be better than ever before.

By following the advice in this book, you will be able to present your book to the right editor at the right publishing house, as professionally as any agent. You will write, talk, think, and act like a professional author and agent. When you respond to an offer from an editor, you will do so knowledgeably. When you and your lawyer negotiate your contract you will know what to reasonably expect.

Would you like someone to do all the things the professional literary agent does? Of course you would. Now, with what you will learn, you can be that someone. And with all your talent and determination, and with this book at your side, you can *Be Your Own Literary Agent*.

I consider this book not only a benefit to you, the author, but of equal service to editors. It is often overlooked that in publishing, editors must discover and develop new authors. The editors who responded to the survey told us that they have, despite incredible odds, discovered and successfully published books submitted by unpublished authors, without an agent. My hope is that soon it will be *your* book the editor finds and publishes, and that it is successful ... and that the time we spend together in the pages that follow helps to make this possible.

Good luck.

Martin P. Levin

1 Selling the First Book: Stories of the Rich and Famous

■ Although it is regrettable that most agents are not available to the unpublished writer, literally thousands of authors have sold their first book on their own. You can take courage from the knowledge that some of the authors whom you probably know very well sold their first book without an agent.

Consider the events surrounding Tom Clancy and his first book, *The Hunt for Red October*, which he wrote during his spare time while working in his family's insurance agency. Clancy had written a short article about the MX missile for Naval Institute Press, a technical publisher affiliated with the Naval Academy. He submitted the manuscript of *The Hunt for Red October*, on his own, without an agent, directly to the editor at the Naval Institute Press seeking "a professional opinion" for his novel-in-progress. Luckily, Naval Institute Press had just decided to try publishing fiction and Clancy's novel had a strong nonfiction angle—the pursuit of a renegade silent submarine. *The Hunt for Red October* was accepted without an agent and became Naval Institute's first published work of fiction. Despite a small first printing and a limited sales effort from a publisher naive in the ways of trade publishing, Tom Clancy's hardcover book became a startling success.

After the book gained public notice, Rena Wolner, president of

Berkley Books, a major paperback publisher, spotted the book, recognized the uniqueness of the approach and the quality of the writing, and bought not only the paperback rights for *The Hunt for Red October* from Naval Institute Press but the rights to all subsequent books as well. It was only at this point that an agent, Robert Gottlieb, was engaged by Clancy. Gottlieb negotiated a $3-million hardcover/softcover deal with Putnam Berkley. When asked if he was surprised Clancy says, "I was thunderstruck, dumbfounded, bowled over, amazed. But I was not surprised." Clancy still works one day a week at the insurance office but says, "It is hard to get worked up over a homeowner's policy nowadays."

Sudden success for unagented authors also happens in the non-fiction field. Robert Coles was a young Air Force doctor stationed in Mississippi in the late 1950s. He was a pediatrician with additional training in child psychology. Peter Davison, an editor at Little, Brown, was impressed by his first article, "A Young Psychiatrist Looks at His Profession," which appeared in *Atlantic Monthly* in 1959. He contacted Coles to see if he'd like to write a book on the subject. That first book led to more than fifty others, which range from studies of children (two of which won the Pulitzer Prize) to biographies and books of selected essays. Modestly, Robert Coles explains that while he does not have "the novelist's gift ... I have that set of mind ... and the novelist's sensibility: to show, not to tell." He has handled all these publishing deals without an agent.

One of the most charming stories of discovery concerns Pat Conroy, author of the very successful *The Prince of Tides* and four other novels. While most authors would be pleased to have one book made into a motion picture, Conroy has had three: *The Prince of Tides*, *The Great Santini*, and *The Water is Wide* (made into the film *Conrack*). Pat Conroy (hard to believe but true) self-published his first book, *The Boo*. Conroy tells the story: "I went to Willie Shepherd at the People's Bank of Beaufort and said, 'Willie, I've written this book about the Citadel and I would like to borrow some money to get it published.' He said, 'Sure, Bubba, how much do you need?' I said, 'Fifteen hundred dollars.' He gave it to me. So I thought I had discovered the secret of getting your books published. I said to myself, 'This is easier than I thought. I think I will be a writer.' "

When Conroy finished his next book, *The Water Is Wide*, an autobiographical work about teaching underprivileged black children on Dawfuskie Island off the South Carolina coast, Willie Shepherd could not finance the book. Someone suggested Conroy call Julian Bach, a distinguished agent in New York City. When he called Bach, Conroy recalls, the agent said, "I am so tired of people like you who call me every day. I don't know why I am talking to you. Send it up and I'll read it when I get some time."

The manuscript was in longhand. Since he could not type, Conroy enlisted the help of his friends in Beaufort, each of whom typed one chapter over the weekend on whatever paper was available. The final manuscript was on a variety of paper, long and short, lined and unlined, hard and onionskin.

Some time later, Julian Bach called Conroy. The conversation, as recollected by Conroy, went like this:

Bach: *Pat, Houghton Mifflin, one of the oldest publishing companies, wants to publish your book. Here's the really good part, $7,500.*

Conroy: *Julian, I don't think Willie Shepherd down at the People's Bank is going to lend me $7,500.*

Bach: *Pat, you realize they pay you the money?*

Conroy learned quickly, but before he would allow Julian Bach to represent him, he wrote, "Dear Mr. Bach: Who are you? I never heard of you. You're an agent? What exactly do you do? Have you ever done this work before?"

Julian Bach responded and Conroy now remembers sheepishly that Bach provided a history of his agency with a client list that included the estate of Charles Dickens and authors such as John

Fowles, the distinguished novelist, and Theodore White, the best-selling writer of nonfiction. Conroy is still represented by Julian Bach.

As evidence that unagented first books can be sold in genres other than adult fiction and nonfiction, author and illustrator Patricia Polacco published her fifteenth children's book in April 1993. She sold her first book on her own. Ms. Polacco's professional publishing career began in 1987, when she was forty-one. She had always created artistic greeting cards for friends to celebrate occasions. A friend encouraged her to form a local chapter of the Society of Children's Book Writers and Illustrators. For about a year she prepared work to share with the group. Ms. Polacco said to her friends, "The whole experience set my pants on fire, and I realized, 'By golly, I think maybe I am going to do this for real.' " Shortly thereafter, in 1987, accompanied by her mother and carrying an eighty-pound portfolio, she saw sixteen publishers in one week and sold her first book, *Meteor*, which is still in print.

Scratch an author and a story of the struggle to get a start emerges. There is always that first published article, novel, children's book, or book of poetry. In the beginning, you must realize, none of the great or not-so-great authors spring full-grown from Minerva's brow or are welcomed by publishers with open arms into the literary fraternity. They trod the road you will tread—as an unagented author in search of a publisher. They succeeded and you will too.

In the process, these now successful authors suffered rejections, which are an upsetting part of the publishing experience. For example, e. e. cummings' poetry was rejected more than a dozen times until it was finally published by his mother. Irving Stone's first book, *Lust for Life*, the story of Vincent Van Gogh, has now sold about twenty million copies. But it was rejected by Knopf, which never even opened the parcel, and fifteen other publishers before it was published by Doubleday. Stephen King, currently America's most prolific and successful contemporary author, had seven novels rejected before *Carrie* was published by Doubleday.

In 1964, a book that added a concept and a phrase to the

American language, *The Peter Principle: Why Things Always Go Wrong*, was rejected by McGraw-Hill. The editor's letter said, "I can see no commercial possibilities for such a book and can consequently offer no encouragement." Thirty publishers rejected the book until William Morrow adventurously paid $2,500 for the manuscript and printed ten thousand copies. The book sold more than two hundred thousand copies in its first year, remained on the best-seller list for a year, and has been translated into thirty-eight languages.

There are thousands* of stories like this of rejection and success. All of them have several common themes. In every instance, there is an author who is determined to write, to be published, and to reach an audience. Harlan Ellison, the novelist who in three decades of work has had forty-five books and fourteen hundred stories, essays, articles, and columns published, says, "There are the poor damaged souls who must write, who haven't any more choice in the matter than whether or not they breathe." In most instances, the author has adhered to the admonition to retain her full-time day job before making writing a career. Sometimes the writers have been teachers, not necessarily of writing, and worked in a nurturing environment that provided time to build a writing career.

In 1974, New American Library acquired paperback rights to *Carrie*, Stephen King's first published novel, from Doubleday for $200,000. As chairman of NAL, I was the host at a lunch in King's honor. I sat next to his wife, Tabitha, and asked her, "What does this first major money mean to you and Stephen?" She replied, "I hope Steve can stop teaching and concentrate on writing." And so he did.

These are but a few of the war stories that authors tell of their

---

* If, after rejection, you wish to have your ego restored, I suggest reading *Writing for Your Life*, edited by Sybil Steinberg (Pushcart Press, 1992) and *On Being a Writer*, edited by Bill Strickland (published by Writers Digest, reprinted in paperback in 1992). And for fun, also read *Rotten Rejections*, edited by André Bernard (Pushcart Press, 1990), over one hundred letters of rejections written to authors who later became world famous.

early struggles. Their purpose here is to give you perspective, determination to continue writing, and fuel for your drive to succeed.

However you are occupied now, if writing is your passion and you have the talent and tenacity, you, like thousands before you, can find a publisher. Talent alone is not enough. Sometimes the tenacious get there faster than those with more talent and less tenacity. Be encouraged and stay positive. Selling your first book takes knowledge, which it is hoped this book will provide. It also takes a strong ego to withstand rejection and persevere. Remember, the editor who rejects your manuscript is not rejecting you but your work, and is challenging you to make it better. You need an editor, but remember, she needs you as well. The discovery of a new publishable author is a coup for an editor, whose advancement depends on her eye for spotting new talent and developing them into publishable authors. This is a symbiotic relationship in which each is nourished by the other. Every author, no matter how successful she is now, had to find a publisher for her first book. Find the editor who needs you as much as you need her, and you become a self-agented, published author.

2 Making Your Book the Best It Can Be

■ The most important talent of a good agent (and the one you must develop) is his ability to look at a work dispassionately and determine if, in his opinion, it is publishable. The reason some publishers will only read agented books is that they depend upon the editorial savvy of the agent, who acts as a screening device. Spouses and significant others can advise you on many things, but the quality of your work and the efficacy of your presentation to the publisher is outside their field of competence and they often lack objectivity. As your own agent, you must find outside counsel to reinforce or revise your judgment that the work you are submitting to the publisher is of sufficient quality to encourage the editor to read your proposal and your sample chapter, and then become excited by your work.

There are many ways to get this counsel, starting with an internal checklist. Ask yourself: Is the subject or the theme of the book one in which I believe passionately? Is it an original concept, or at least a fresh approach to an established theme? Is it a subject that I know enough about to make an interesting and useful book? Is there a need for this book? How many people will be interested in my idea? Is there enough depth for a book, or is it a magazine article? (A book, unlike an article, must have scope and sufficient well-developed detail, which adds significantly to the reader's information and enjoyment.) If you can answer "yes" to these questions, all else being equal, you should be able to write a substantial and salable book and, with a professional marketing plan and proposal, sell it to a publisher. In Chapter 5, you will be taken behind the closed doors of publishing houses, introduced to editors who are likely to read your manuscript, and listen to them discuss their criteria for a book they are likely to acquire. As you will see, the overwhelming response from the editorial assistants who read unsolicited manuscripts is about the lack of quality and professionalism in the submissions.

One of the most common faults I have seen over the years is the attempt by the novice author to seek out an idea "that has never been done before." If the idea has not been done before (and this is doubtful), there is probably a good reason for it. A first-time author, or one who wishes to move his career along, is better served by writing a more intriguing mystery, a well-developed romance, or a better how-to book. The most exciting example of "doing it better" is Martha Stewart, who is now an industry unto herself with seven published books, a cooking school, a magazine bearing her name, and a television career.

Martha was the wife of Andrew Stewart, who worked with me at the Times Mirror publishing group. She is a superb cook, and she loves crafts, antiques, gardening, and entertaining. When I first met her, she was a stockbroker facing a layoff because of declining business in the brokerage house for which she worked. During her down time, Martha wrote a book called *Entertaining*, which combined fresh and delicious recipes and excellent illustrations with beautiful, creative ideas on being a good hostess. She tested all the recipes in her own kitchen, supervised the photography, and wrote about how to present the right foods in the right social setting. She convinced Crown Publishers to publish her first book, which has now sold over five hundred thousand copies and has continued to create a veritable library of her best-selling books in this genre.

Martha Stewart moved into a crowded field, but she was passionate about her love for food and entertaining. She had an innovative approach, knew her subject in depth, knew that millions of people cared about the subjects she chose, and knew that she could interest them in her work.

Shari Lewis, now appearing successfully on her own PBS program, is passionate about her love for children, songs, and stories. Her career began when her husband, publisher Jeremy Tarcher, encouraged her during their honeymoon to write a book she sold on the basis of a title *How to Pull Strings and Influence Puppets*. (Shari began her professional career as a puppeteer after having been sidelined from her dancing career by an injury.)

Shari's writing career, which began in 1958, becomes more successful every year. Among her best-sellers for parents and children is a series of "One Minute Bedtime Stories." From the beginning, with scores of books, tapes, records, and videos to her credit, Shari has been her own agent. I have known Shari and published some of her early books, always dealing directly with her, and she is an effective agent for her own work. She has said, "For writers in particular, I think the best advice anyone can give is to be critical about your work until you're done."

Before you expose your book to professional editors, do a reality check of your own. Find published books in a genre similar to yours and ask yourself, "Is what I have written as good as this published book, or better?" This is the first level of the reality check. If you feel you can improve your sample chapter, do it before you submit it to a publisher. Some writers will submit a manuscript saying, "I know this needs work, but I thought you could tell me what to do." If you know it needs work, do the work first and submit it with confidence. If you are not sure of the quality, how can an editor ever be enthusiastic about reading it? If you feel any part of your sample chapter or presentation can be improved, do so before you submit it. The best way to improve your odds of being accepted is by offering a quality product confidently.

Recently, I was working with a nationally known businessman and his collaborating writer to test the market for a book he wished to write. The concept was outstanding, the outline was good, but the sample chapter was a disaster. The organization was so poor that the material was inaccessible to the reader. The chapter needed a sharper focus that would reveal the excellent concept. I refused to include the sample chapter in the presentation and stopped interviews with major publishers until it was rewritten.

It was amazing that the author, a top-notch chief executive officer who was well read and had an excellent critical sense, did not know that what he had written was not publishable. The poor judgment of the professional writer and collaborator was even more amazing. Somehow, they believed the idea would override the shoddy work in the sample chapter. Not so. To be successful in the highly competitive arena of publishing, you must be the best you can be. Quality counts.

If you are part of a writers working group, your fellow writers may be able to provide constructive criticism of your work. They may not have the best quality or most authoritative advice, but it may help you think about how the public may react to your work and what needs to be done to improve your manuscript. If you can spend the time and money to attend a writers workshop where you can get the help of a professional teacher and critic, do it. The *Guide to Writers Conferences*, 4th edition ($18.95, from Shaw Guides, 625 Biltmore Way, Suite 1406, Coral Gables, FL 33134) lists and describes 344 conferences, 35 residences and retreats, and 114 writers' organizations in 45 states and 11 countries.

Some of the most useful one-on-one criticism of your writing may come from freelance editors or "book doctors" who offer editorial services for a fee. There are twenty pages of names, addresses, and specialties in the doorstop-sized directory of American publishing, *Literary Market Place* (published annually by R. R. Bowker, and available for about $170; every good library should have one). These editors, many former editors of major publishing houses and some retired editors-in-chief, will review your letter, proposal, and sample chapter, and even complete your manuscript, for a fee. You can identify the service you want by reading the entries listed in *LMP*, in sections labeled Editorial Services and/or Editorial Consultants. You will find descriptions such as:

"analyses of manuscripts"

"manuscript evaluation"

"book proposal development"

These phrases may lead you to the right person to help you. When you write or telephone, however, determine if you and the individual are compatible, if his background is suitable for your project, and if you can afford the fee. Jerry Gross, with whom I worked when he was Editor-in-Chief of New American Library, has written an excellent, helpful essay, "Working With a Free-Lance Editor or Book Doctor," which appears in his book, *Editors on Editing*.

Why the emphasis on quality? As an unpublished author or an author unhappy with her progress, you are trying to beat incredible odds in publishing. Publishers receive thousands of manuscripts directly from authors without any solicitation. These are called "unsolicited manuscripts" and are dumped in one place, which has an unfortunate name: the Slush Pile. Not even a Las Vegas book-maker would quote the odds on an unsolicited manuscript being removed from the Slush Pile and being read, let alone being accepted. You must do all you can to avoid this fate. But take heart: many of the unsolicited and unagented books that pour in to publishers *are* read, usually in a rush. That is why before you expose yourself to this risky, long, and difficult process, the quality of your work should be the very best it can be. Self-analysis, writers groups, retreats, and outside help do not guarantee success, but they will improve the odds, making you more confident of the quality of your work, and thus more persistent in seeking a publisher, because you will have been advised that your book is publishable. After you become a published author, your editor will suggest the direction you should take in your next work and provide the criticism you need to be even more successful.

With a professionally competent manuscript, if you follow the Eight-Step Program discussed in the next chapter, it is possible to improve the odds on your manuscript avoiding the Slush Pile, being read, and being accepted for publication.

3 The Eight-Step Program for Selling Your Book

■ It is difficult to shift gears from being the creative artist to being the seller of one's work, but this is a part of the real-life experience of a first-time author. *Literary Market Place* has more than two hundred pages of publishers' listings. According to recent government and private studies, it is estimated that there are more than thirty-six hundred publishers in the United States who publish three or more books annually. The challenge remains: to develop a selling strategy, to find the right publisher and the right editor, and to negotiate a successful deal, finalized by a fair contract.

If you follow this eight-step program, you can be your own agent—successfully. Here is an overview of the program.

1. Write a Winning Proposal. This will attract attention and present your work in the best possible light.

In Hollywood, screenwriters make their "pitch" to potential producers in person. They generate interest by presenting a "high concept," a shorthand form of telling the story in an intriguing manner in one or two sentences, hopefully eliciting interest in hearing the story in its entirety. Once the studio is attracted to the idea, the writer is asked to present a short summary and, if acceptable, is engaged to write the screenplay. With a few variations, this is the same basic process that is used in publishing. Your cover letter to the editor must contain a "high concept," crisply stated in a sentence or two, which introduces a carefully crafted proposal that includes a summary of your book, one or two sample chapters, and, for nonfiction, a table of contents. This technique is discussed in Chapter 6, and a wide variety of sample letters and proposals is provided in Chapter 7.

2. Find the Best Publisher. Publishers specialize—even conglomerates (the super-publishers) separate the company into separate divisions and imprints, some devoted to specialized areas of publishing. For example, an author with a romance novel probably would and should seek out Harlequin, the world's largest publisher of romance novels. However, since romance novels now comprise almost half of all popular mass market literature sold, many other publishers are in the market, including New American Library, Warner, Pocket, Bantam, Berkley, Avon, Dell, and Zebra Books. All publish romance novels. There are also smaller publishers, such as Leisure, that buy romance novels. You increase your odds of being published by identifying publishers who are most likely to be interested in the subject of your manuscript. How can you find these publishers?

Literary Market Place is the most authoritative source to help you match your book to a potential publisher. Its weakness is its lack of subjective opinion, a fault remedied by *Writer's Market*, published annually by Writer's Digest Books. This is a good source of publisher listings (though not so extensive—about 900), and includes extra information valuable to the first-time author, such as how often the house buys unagented works, range of advances, and so on. Jeff Herman's *Insider's Guide to Book Editors, Publishers, and Literary Agents* (updated annually) is also good, though it has fewer listings; its chief advantage is its listings of individual editors (and their areas of expertise) at several hundred of the larger trade houses, and a detailed description of each publisher. Herman also has separate sections for university publishers and religious publishers. How to find the *right* publisher is addressed more fully in Chapter 4.

3. Submit Your Book to the Right Editor. This is by far the most difficult task. While some publishers announce they will not accept unagented manuscripts, the survey I conducted reveals that editors at most of these houses will take a peek at unagented works. Not much of a peek, but a peek. Write to the editor by name. In a recent lecture at the Stanford Professional Publishing Course, at which I teach each year, a leading editor said, "If an author takes the trouble to find out about me and writes a personal letter to me, I will respond." I would surmise that many dedicated editors feel the same way. Besides, all editors dream of finding a new best-seller in an unsolicited manuscript. In Chapter 5, I describe in detail how to find the right editor—and what she does when the manuscript is received.

4. Use the Two P's—Patience and Persistence. Once the proposal is in the mail, there is an anxious waiting period which is usually longer than the author expects. Our survey, reported in Chapter 5, tells you "What Goes on Behind Closed Doors." Once a suitable time has passed, a follow-up, which *might* send someone to the Slush Pile to find your buried letter, outline, and sample chapter, is in order. Publishers rarely review unsolicited manuscripts on a regular schedule. Suitable time may mean as little as thirty days and as long as six months—and these delays require persistence and patience. A follow-up after sixty days is appropriate.

5. Use the Rejection Profitably. In some instances, the rejected manuscript is accompanied by a form letter. If the form letter has a signature, this is a contact to be exploited. Editors will occasionally talk to authors of unsolicited manuscripts. Sometimes when they reject a manuscript, editors write a *real* letter with helpful comments. A long rejection letter can often shed light on why your manuscript is not being bought. In either case, when you receive a rejection letter with an editor's name shown, you have made progress in finding someone who might discuss your manuscript with you.

If you can get through to the editor who read your submission, the questions you might ask are:

- If I improve the work as you suggested, is this the type of manuscript that your house might publish?
- What are your editorial guidelines?
- If this book is not suitable for your house, do you have suggestions as to who might be a publisher in this area?
- Do you have the name of someone at a house that is publishing in this area to whom I can write?
- Was the proposal inviting? Are there areas I could improve?
- Did the sample chapter(s) effectively display my ability and professionalism?
- Is there someone I could contact who might be able to work with me?
- Is there an agent whom you could recommend who might take me as a client? May I use your name as a reference?

If you are fortunate enough to get a "glowing" rejection, one in which the editor says that you "show promise," the major question to be asked is, "Do you have any specific suggestions that would help me make my book good enough for you to acquire it?"

6. Keep Moving. Network. Find Places in Which You Can Make Contact with Publishers and Editors. Since you are trying to move from being Mr. or Ms. Anonymous to being a real person in the world of publishing, you need to make contact with real publishers and editors. As was mentioned previously, there are 344 conferences, workshops, and seminars sponsored by colleges, universities, libraries, and cultural organizations. These conferences are held in forty-five states and eleven countries. Normally these conferences extend from two to four days and are attended by aspiring writers or published authors who are looking for current information about trends, editors, and marketing tips. The faculty for these conferences are working professionals from large and small publishers, editors, agents, or established authors.

Some of the writers conferences also offer individual critical appraisal of attendees' works-in-progress. The fees vary according to the length of the conference and range from $100 to $400 or more. There should be a meeting close to your home and one, it is hoped, that you can afford.

If you cannot attend a workshop, there are forty writers organizations that conduct regular meetings and provide networking opportunities. Their fees are nominal and they are designed to support and encourage the writer.

For published writers or other serious writers who find it difficult to write with the distractions of their current environment, there are thirty-five residences and retreats. These places are not elegant. The rooms are sparsely furnished and inexpensive. There are common halls for meals and meetings where you can make contacts. (Many retreats require the applicant to submit a sample of published work or work-in-progress.)

The Guide to Writers Conferences is the book that lists all these opportunities. In it, you will find descriptions of the available programs, schedules, faculty credentials, application requirements, living facilities, and costs, all well presented.

Beyond this, to keep up to date, you should attend, if possible, the annual trade exhibit of the American Booksellers Association. It is held each year, usually at the end of May or the beginning of June, and almost every publisher in America attends. At this trade show, you will see the books publishers will be offering for the upcoming fall season and some previously published books. In a single location, you get a sense of what each publisher is publishing. You will also get a good picture of where your book fits. Many editors attend the ABA, and you might be able to get a few moments of conversation, if you are polite and persistent. Even more important, the ABA Trade Exhibition is attended by hundreds of smaller publishers, where you can meet the owner or the publisher—the real decision-makers in these companies.

If you cannot afford to visit the ABA trade show, which is held in Chicago, you should attend one of the regional exhibitions which are held in cities throughout the United States. Fewer publishers attend, but the regional shows have all the benefits, on a smaller scale, of the ABA. (The smaller size will also increase your chances of personal contact.) All of these exhibitions and their locations are listed in *Publishers Weekly*, the trade magazine of the book industry, well before the event.

7. Think Small. Do not be afraid to consider alternatives to one of the large New York publishers. Some of your best chances of having your manuscript read by a decision-maker are with a small publisher, many of whom are located outside New York City. Many of these "small" publishers, because they have been willing to read unsolicited manuscripts and work with first-time authors, have become medium-sized, profitable, and admired in the profession. As I've mentioned previously, there are more than thirty-six hundred trade publishers in the United States. Most literary agents concentrate, for obvious reasons (mainly financial), on the largest two dozen. Consequently, small and midsized publishers work with un-agented authors for three main reasons: (1) they don't have the money to shell out for advances that the big publishers have; (2) the Big Book/Big Author Syndrome is not as important to them; and (3) they have to—they'd never find enough books within their budget to publish if they didn't.

To assist you, I have created a personal list of Best Bets—small and midsized publishers where your chances of being noticed and talking to an editor, or even the publisher himself, are greater than at the major houses. You will find scores of publishers listed. You can add publishers to this list through your own experience. Since addresses may change, check with the latest edition of *LMP* before mailing material. Small and midsized publishers who value new authors will read unsolicited manuscripts, and they are more likely to risk publishing a first-time author. Think small. There is time, if you feel it is necessary, after your first published book, to think big.

8. Keep Reading. Being a writer and an agent is a continuing effort, and you should do what literary agents do: read *Publishers Weekly* every week. It is the "bible" for the publishing industry. Publishers advertise and *PW* extensively reviews forthcoming books, which will give you a sense of what is coming to the market and of developing trends. Major personnel changes are reported; this information updates the entries in *LMP* so your letter will be properly addressed. And, from time to time, there are excellent articles which describe the market for each of the categories of publishing. Current and back issues of *Publishers Weekly* can be found in most public libraries.

For general background on the publishing scene, read the *New York Times Book Review*, *Time*, or *Newsweek*, or the book review section that appears in your local newspaper. *Writer's Digest* is a monthly magazine that regularly runs updated market reports and frequently lists publishers, editors, and agents and what they're looking for.

The Eight-Step Program for Selling Your Book

To recap:

1. Write a Winning Proposal.
2. Find the Best Publisher.
3. Find the Right Editor.
4. Use the Two P's—Patience and Persistence.
5. Use Rejections Profitably.
6. Keep Moving. Make Contacts. Network.
7. Think Small.
8. Keep Reading.

The effective, professional, full-time agent uses this program; he knows, or thinks he knows, the right publisher and editor to get a sympathetic reading. He helps his client improve her proposal. He knows how long to wait before following up. If there is a rejection, the agent seeks the editor's advice for improvement. Where indicated, agents will make submissions to midsized and small publishers if they believe they can get a more sympathetic reading of the manuscript there. A good agent is always on the move, keeps up to date, and knows the specialized publishers who might buy the book he is selling. When you follow this eight-step program, you will be able to do virtually everything the professional agent does to sell his client's book. With practice, you might even do it better.

4   Finding the Best Publisher for Your Book

■ The publishing industry has become very complex over the last four decades. Hardcover publishers own mass market houses. Publishers of professional books also publish trade books. Almost all publishers create what the industry calls trade paperbacks, a softcover version of the hardcover book. About half of all mass market paperback books never appear in hardcover, but are published as paperback originals. Each type of book dictates a different submission strategy. Without knowing your manuscript, it is difficult to pinpoint how to market your book. Use this chapter as a road map to lead you to the category in which your book would fall.

1. The Trade Book
2. The Mass Market Paperback
3. The Juvenile Book
4. The Professional Book
5. The Scholarly and University Press Book
6. The Subscription Reference Book
7. The Elementary or High School Textbook
8. The College Textbook
9. The Religious Book

Once you find the category in which your manuscript falls, you are on the way to finding the best publisher for your book.

To do your own agenting successfully and to find the best publisher, you need a clear picture of how publishing is organized—and how complex it has become. As so often happens in publishing, there are significant exceptions to every rule. A publisher may be listed in one category, but may also publish in others. This chapter will help you understand the regularities and identify some of the exceptions.

The Trade Book

Trade books are hardcover books and trade paperbacks (the larger full-sized paperback, not the rack-sized mass market ones) designed for the general consumer and sold for the most part in bookstores. Public libraries are also major customers for trade books. In some instances trade books are sold to libraries and schools for classroom use. Many trade book houses have juvenile divisions, publishing hardcover and paperback books for children.

Included in the trade book category are books of fiction, non-fiction, biography, classics, cooking, history, popular science, travel, and art. You will also find trade books that help in learning a foreign language and "how to" books that guide the reader in participating in sports, music, poetry, and drama. The categories of non-fiction are virtually limitless.

Some book publishers have a narrow focus. Generally speaking, the smaller the publisher, the tighter the focus. The clearest example is Fielding, a publisher that sells travel books exclusively. But most of the largest trade book publishers produce fiction and non-fiction books, hardcover and trade paperbacks, adult and juvenile books. The names of these trade book companies are well known, and most of them are deeply involved in multiple areas of publishing. You will recognize the names of Simon & Schuster, Random House, and Doubleday, to name a few.

Trade paperback books, once a rarity, have become a staple of the industry, and virtually every hardcover house publishes them. They are usually the same size or slightly smaller than the original hardcover editions, unlike the much smaller mass market paperbacks. Trade paperbacks are sold primarily in book stores. Because of the popularity of the format, trade paperbacks vary in size and are designated paperbacks chiefly due to their specialized content and higher prices. Their sales and distribution practices and returns policies adhere to those of their hardcover brethren, not their mass market relatives.

You must be aware of who publishes what. There are six levels of research to determine whether a particular trade publishing house publishes books in your genre:

1. Use *LMP*. You can start by consulting *Literary Market Place*, which lists every publisher, large and small. In *LMP* there is (1) an alphabetical listing of publishers (which includes the names of executives and editors for each house), and (2) a list of publishers by subject area. Use the alphabetical and category lists to find a specific publisher. If you are interested in locating a publisher of juvenile books, for instance, *LMP*'s category index provides a list of all publishers of "Juvenile and Young Adult Books." Here you will find, for example, HarperCollins listed as a publisher in this category. You would then look up HarperCollins in the alphabetical index located in the front section of *LMP* to get the address, telephone number, and fax number for HarperCollins. There you will also find the names of the publisher, editorial directors, and editors. The listing in *LMP* also provides the number of titles in print and the annual number of titles published. This can be used to measure publishing activity. The date the company was founded is also shown, and measures its longevity and possibly its stability. You should be able to find the house you seek and the name of an editor to whom you can write. Be aware, though, that editors move from publisher to publisher, so always call and check *before* sending your manuscript.

The list of potential publishers for your book will probably be too large initially, and you should refine the list by following steps 2 through 6 below.

2. Write for a Catalog. Once you have finished your initial search, write to the address shown in *LMP*, attention "Customer Service," asking for a catalog of new and backlisted titles. By studying the catalog, you will get a feel for whether or not your book would fit into the publisher's program. This should enable you to eliminate some of the names you found in *LMP* and narrow your target list.

3. Visit a Library, Bookstore, or Trade Show. Visit your library (if you are not already there using *LMP*) or a bookstore, where you can find the books published by a house that you believe may be a potential buyer of your manuscript. Visit a bookstore, especially a "superstore," where from fifty thousand to one hundred thousand titles from all publishers will be on display. If it is a quiet time in the bookstore, a knowledgeable clerk can tell you a great deal about the publisher and his books. And since most bookstores are organized by categories, the shelves will contain most of the current published books in the genre in which you are interested. Check to see which publishers operate in your category. If you attend the ABA or any other trade show, you will be able to see the books publishers plan to release in the next season. This investigation will give you an excellent idea of the category of books likely to be of interest to a publisher.

4. Try to Meet a Publisher's Sales Representative. If you are very lucky when you are at the bookstore, you might run into the salesperson for the publisher. You are more likely to find him at a trade show. The sales "rep" is an excellent source of information for you. He can tell you if your book fits within the category of the books his house publishes. He knows his list and his competitors' lists and which books and categories sell. If asked, the salesperson might be able to give you the name of the editor to whom you should send your proposal, and he can provide valuable insight as to the books the publisher is likely to accept.

5. Check *Books in Print*. All nonfiction (and fiction) books are listed in the annual directory *Books in Print*. Most libraries have *Books in Print* in the reference section. A check of the listings will reveal those books similar to your book, and who published them. This is a valuable tool—especially the Subject Guide, which will help you find the titles of published books that might compete with your manuscript. There are volumes of *Books in Print* that list paperback books and forthcoming books, and provide book reviews.

When you compare your manuscript to books already published, you can determine how your book differs. Most editors who read nonfiction manuscripts are impressed when you tell them how your book compares with books previously published—it shows you've done a professional job of researching the competition and the market for your book, and will cast you in a favorable light.

6. Find the Right Editor. At the end of this process, you should have created a list of publishers in your category, narrowed them down, studied their lists, and obtained the address and name of the right editor to whom to write from the listing in *LMP*. (Another method: check the acknowledgments in a book like yours. More often than not, an author will thank her editor by name.)

Always write to a specific editor. It may be difficult with limited knowledge to select the right editor, and publishing is known for its high turnover rate. If you write to the wrong or a long-gone editor, your proposal will usually be forwarded to the correct editor, but why take that chance? It's best always to confirm information by phone. Ask the editorial assistant who is likely to answer the phone if your contact name is correct and, if not, who is the person who edits books like yours.

Your objective is to send your proposal to the *right* editor at the *right* publishing house. Follow these steps and your odds of success will increase greatly.

The Mass Market Paperback

Since over 50 percent of all mass market paperbacks are books originally written for paperback publication without a prior hardcover, this is a significant market for authors. Proposals for books that are likely to be published as "paperback originals" should be submitted directly to the paperback publisher. However, the market has become complicated, since gradually, over the last two decades, most of the larger hardcover publishers have acquired or developed their own mass market paperback companies. The following are several examples:

Bantam and Dell have a single owner, Bertelsmann. Each of these companies has independent editorial departments, and each will buy hardcover and paperback rights.

HarperCollins, a venerable trade publisher, has its own mass market paperback entity, Harper Paperbacks.

Avon (paperback) is owned by Hearst and affiliated with Morrow (hardcover trade paperback) but operates for the most part independently.

Penguin (hardcover, paperback), New American Library (hardcover, paperback), Dutton (hardcover, trade paperback), and Viking (hardcover) are owned by Pearson, Ltd. and operate as Penguin USA, with one executive directing all the subsidiaries and divisions, each of which has a great deal of independence and separate editorial departments.

Putnam Publishing Group publishes an extensive line of hardcover and trade paperbacks under the Putnam, Grosset, and Jeremy P. Tarcher imprints. Putnam also publishes mass market books under the Berkley banner, and how-to and children's books under the Price Stern Sloan, Grosset & Dunlap, and Putnam imprints. Each entity acquires books independently.

Random House owns the mass market paperback houses Ballantine, Fawcett, and Del Rey. Here, too, the paperback publishers have separate editorial departments.

Simon and Schuster, a diversified trade publisher with a major presence, owns Pocket Books (paperbacks) and Collier Books (trade paperbacks). In addition, this $2 billion giant has a wide variety of imprints with separate editorial departments.

St. Martin's Press publishes hardcover, trade paperback, and mass market titles in many subject areas.

Time Warner, with major interests in magazines and books, owns Warner Books, which publishes in hardcover, trade paperback, and mass market, and Little Brown, which is a hardcover and trade paperback publisher.

Zebra Books and its recent acquisition, Pinnacle Books, publish a large list of mass market originals and occasional hardcover and trade titles.

In submitting a manuscript to those publishers with both hardcover and paperback divisions, you should submit your book to the hardcover imprint, unless it is the type of book that is rarely published in hardcover—for example, romance novels, westerns, or travel books. In some instances, the hardcover publisher will endeavor to buy hardcover, trade paperback, and mass paperback rights. In other instances, when the hardcover publisher feels he can get a larger sum of money for paperback rights by selling them to an external company, he will retain the rights and sell them, after hardcover publication, to the highest bidder.

A first-time author submitting a book to the largest houses (those that publish about 70 percent of the titles in the trade and mass market areas) must be careful to select the right subsidiary or division, and then identify the editor to whom the book should be submitted. *LMP* will help because it lists the imprints (divisions within a publishing house) and the editors of each imprint, but, if you are in doubt about which imprint to approach, call the publisher's promotion department. If you are lucky, one of the assistants will explain the organizational structure. Then, look for the name of the editor shown in *LMP* and call to verify the listing. The question "Does Miss Brown still edit mysteries?" will probably get you the information you need.

The Juvenile Book

The juvenile book market will soon reach $1 billion in sales. Many trade book companies have a line of juvenile books and acquire these books in the same manner that they acquire trade books. Agents are more likely to represent established authors, while unpublished authors submit their manuscripts directly to the publisher. Illustrators are often represented by agents but some carry their work around in portfolios to show editors, when they can get an appointment. There are many literary agents who specialize in representing authors of juvenile books.

One of the main factors in the boom of the juvenile market is the growth of publishers who publish only for this market. Scholastic, a very large publisher of hardcover and paperback books sold to the trade, with book clubs for schools, book fairs, films, and audio, is now the dominant publisher in juvenile publishing. There are many other publishers who publish only juvenile books such as Millbrook Press, Troll Books, and a long list of other independent publishers whose main focus is on the school and library market.

Selling your manuscript in the juvenile market is similar to selling your book to a trade publisher. If you follow the six steps described for trade books (pages 22 to 24), you will be able to find the best publisher and the right editor for your juvenile manuscript. While there has been a significant improvement in the royalty advances paid to the more popular authors and illustrators, the economic terms offered to writers of children's books are significantly less than those offered to writers of adult books. What encourages writers is that the life of a juvenile book is usually far longer than that of an adult book. For those who have the talent, writing for children is still rich and rewarding—and the publishers are often accessible to you without an agent.

The Professional Book

The professional book market is not as complex as the trade market and editors are far more accessible. In this field of publishers, there are three major subdivisions:

1. Technical and Scientific Books, which include subjects in technology, engineering, and the physical, biological, earth, and social sciences. These books are directed at practicing and research scientists, engineers, architects, and other professionals in these fields.

2. Medical Books, written for physicians, nurses, dentists, hospital administrators, and others in human and allied health services.

3. Business and Other Professional Books, addressed to business people, managers, accountants, lawyers, librarians, and other professionals.

Several traditional business publishers have broadened the business category, once restricted to serious professional literature, and now also produce nonfiction books for the general reader, some of which have become commercially successful. Doubleday and HarperCollins both have divisions specializing in popular business books. Your research, as described in the trade book area, will locate all those professional publishers who cater to readers of popular business books.

Unlike trade books, where books are created entirely by outside authors, manuscripts in the traditional professional areas are sometimes originated in house (by the publisher) and developed with the help of outside writers.

In other areas of professional publishing, such as medicine and engineering, for example, authors are sought by editors called "acquisition editors," who attend professional meetings and visit campuses to meet authorities in the field and seek out their manuscripts. Many books are developed from unsolicited manuscripts. An author with an idea for a book in the area of her expertise can usually find an acquisition editor at a convention or meeting who will arrange to review a manuscript. Failing this, she can submit a query letter to the professional publisher's editor-in-chief, who would be listed in *LMP*. Most professionals know the leading publishing houses intimately, since much of their professional reading is published by them. In general, editors in the professional and scientific areas of publishing are often accessible by telephone, especially to professionals, and they are more responsive than editors in the trade areas. The size of this market is substantial; while served by fewer publishers, on a dollar volume basis this area of publishing is roughly equal to the revenues of all trade books. Professional books are not as glamorous as trade books, but they are important to professionals in the United States and throughout the world.

The Scholarly and University Press Book

While some scholarly books are published by not-for-profit entities, research institutes, museums, and learned societies, the university press publishers are the publishers of choice. Their excellent editors often have one eye on the general trade market. There are over one hundred university presses, most of which are members of the American Association of University Presses (AAUP). The largest of the university presses—Harvard, Yale, M.I.T., University of Chicago, Johns Hopkins—have recently become an excellent alternative for authors of serious trade books. This phenomenon has occurred because many of the traditional trade book publishers are publishing fewer serious nonfiction books. Nonetheless, even the aggressive, trade-oriented university presses still publish primarily for the scholarly market. They are a good option for the serious book that may have popular appeal, especially if the hardcover book would ultimately find its way into a trade paperback list, which university presses have and treasure.

LMP lists all of the university presses, along with their editors. However, the American Association of University Presses publishes a more extensive directory with a list of editors and other useful information.*

---

* This directory, which is issued annually, is extraordinarily valuable because it is filled with useful information to help the author submit her manuscript. You can find this book in most libraries or purchase a copy from the Association of American University Presses, Inc., 584 Broadway, New York, NY 10012, or by calling 212-941-6610 or faxing 212-941-6618.

While university presses and other scholarly publishers do not represent a large market, they are ideal for the book that is designed for a specialized, serious market and occasionally for a trade book that will sell to a professional college audience.

University presses maintain a sales staff that sells to university bookstores as well as to general bookstores. When university presses have a book with trade potential, they publish and sell it in much the same manner as a commercial trade publisher.

Subscription Reference Books

Encyclopedias and other reference books have been a major force in publishing, with distinguished sets of books that have been created and revised over the years. Many articles are contributed by writers with special expertise in their field. Since the domestic market for these books has been shrinking, and more work has been moved inside to the salaried staff, this represents a limited and less attractive market for the freelance writer.

Elementary and High School Textbooks

Books serving the elementary and high school markets represent a billion dollars in sales. These books are created by a limited number of publishers, all of which are listed in *LMP*. The major publishers, such as Addison-Wesley, D. C. Heath, Harcourt Brace, ScottForesman (a division of HarperCollins), and Silver Burdett Ginn (a part of Simon & Schuster's empire), control this market. The books and materials are generated internally, but freelancers are often used. How these publishers create elementary textbooks and what they include in their curriculum is often of interest to authors writing popular curriculum-oriented juvenile books. If your juvenile book can be tied to an area of the curriculum, it will have sales potential to schools.

In creating a textbook for the Elementary-High School (El-Hi) market, the publisher, with his staff and expert consultants, sets out a concept or framework for a series of books to be created in a discipline along with supplementary materials to be used in the classroom. Materials for computers, which are becoming more common in schools, are also included in the package to enhance the learning experience.

The publisher then seeks authors who can create the books in the program. These are usually teachers or curriculum specialists who have demonstrated the ability to communicate to the student. Publishers seek out these writers by visiting schools, attending conventions of teachers, and reading the professional press. Authors with educational credentials who have the ability to write books in a manner appropriate for the grade level are sought. Some authors of El-Hi texts are paid modest royalties; most work on a flat-fee basis in which the author receives a fixed payment for her work, without any royalties, on completion of the assignment. For the qualified author, this is an interesting and lucrative market. Rarely is there a need for an author with credentials to use an agent to sell her work.

A far better market for the writer with the skills to write for student audiences is the publisher who develops supplementary books—juvenile books designed to supplement the El-Hi textbook in the classroom. While the authors' earnings are modest, the supplementary books often stay in print for a long period of time and produce steady royalties. The books are written for the El-Hi student, sometimes heavily illustrated (provided separately by the publisher), and are curriculum related. While *LMP* lists the publishers who develop supplementary books, they are more readily identified by visiting a library with a good children's book collection, or by visiting the semiannual American Library Association trade show and the International Reading Association Trade Show. It helps to see firsthand who publishes the kind of books you wish to write rather than just looking at a catalog and a list of publishers. *PW* announces when and where these trade shows take place.

The elementary and high school market is one of several markets that can provide income, experience, and writing credits that are helpful on a curriculum vitae. The writer usually works on a freelance basis under the term of employment "work for hire." This legal term covers the arrangement in which the publisher asks the writer to write a specific piece under his supervision and directions. The writer is usually paid a one-time fee and occasionally a modest royalty. Copyright is held by the publisher, who owns all rights to the book. Working on projects under the direction of a publisher may generate opportunities for the writer of original works to publish them with a division of that publishing house that concentrates on trade juvenile books.

College Textbooks

College publishing is also a major specialized market, changing now with the growing importance of the computer and CD-ROM. Textbooks, for the most part, come from experts in each field. Recently, publishers have created the "managed textbook" in which the publisher sets out the framework for the book and seeks authors to write some or all of the contents. As in the case of El-Hi books, authors are recruited by acquisition editors who read the appropriate literature, attend conventions, and visit schools. Authors need educational credentials (usually a Ph.D.) and must be respected in their field. It is a market limited to the professionals.

An author who feels she has the educational qualifications and something special to offer should send a query letter to the publisher. If the publisher is interested in the subject proposed by the author, she would, as in trade book publishing, follow with a book proposal: a summary, a table of contents, a sample chapter, and a curriculum vitae. The publisher will usually expect the author to do an analysis of the competitive texts in the field to help him make a decision. Unlike trade publishers, the college publisher is usually responsive to a prospective author's inquiry for two reasons: professional courtesy, and a belief that the potential writer, who is usually a professor, might have influence in adopting the books she offers. Rarely does a college text author use or need an agent, and rarely is an advance or royalty important to the author. The prestige associated with a published textbook and the requirements of the profession to "publish or perish" weight the scales in favor of the publisher, who may even require that the author provide illustrations at her own expense.

Religious Books

Included in this publishing area are Bibles, hymnals, and prayer books. These days, this market is not limited to the professional theologian. Many religious houses publish inspirational books of all kinds, including fiction, nonfiction, and poetry, and constitute an excellent market for the qualified author. The tools and techniques for determining the publishers in the market for inspirational books are the same as for trade books.

The market for religious books has broadened. Previously the domain of the denominational houses such as the Baptist Publish House or the Paulist Press, trade publishing houses have entered the field and the traditional religious publishers have also expanded their lists.

Thomas Nelson, a Nashville based publisher, is typical of the religious publisher who now provides new opportunities for authors who can write for the inspirational audience. Nelson grew from a small Bible business into a major factor in religious book and music publishing when it acquired Word, a Dallas based publisher. The Nelson list is dotted with luminaries such as Dale Evans, but also has a place for the new author with an inspirational story to tell.

"Angel books" have become, at least for the present, the religious book best sellers. One publishing house, Barton and Brett, Publishers, Inc., was actually founded to publish *Where Angels Walk*, written by a newly discovered author, Joan Wester Anderson. This book became a major best seller in hardcover and then in paperback. This and other books created a new category in the religious field and has led to successful careers for authors who never before enjoyed major success.

An excellent source for identifying a potential market, such as the religious and inspirational market, is to find a Spring or Fall Books issue of *Publishers Weekly* at your super bookstore or in a local library. This issue of *PW* lists over twenty-five hundred books to be published in the forthcoming season. In the 1994 fall book issue there were thirty-four different publishers who announced new books. By reviewing the lists of forthcoming books organized by category and publisher, you can discover emerging trends and the little-known publishers who may be your best market.

What the Future Holds

The author looking to the future must take note of the computer. In addition, the use of CD-ROM is important. Except for a few outstanding CD-ROMs, individual sales of this multimedia product have been modest. Nevertheless, it is clear that for future success, the modern author must become familiar with new technologies, as she may be called upon to create or adapt material for this market. Once the introduction of these new technologies seemed decades away. Given the dramatic increase in the availability of the computer and CD-ROM players to average people, the future is now. And for those authors who understand computers and new technologies and can write about them clearly, it is a burgeoning new market.

Once you place your book within the publishing framework of a specific segment of the industry, it is possible by a series of inquiries to narrow your search until you find the most likely publishers for your book and the editors to whom you should send your proposal. This overview of publishing should help you realize that you have more publishing options than you first imagined; your publisher of choice might be other than a traditional trade publisher. By understanding the book industry and its areas of concentration, you can improve your targeting and find the *right* publisher for your book. You might even find a market for your book you might otherwise have overlooked. Remember: hunting for the right publisher is best done using a rifle rather than a shotgun.

5 What Goes on behind Closed Doors

■ Who is that mysterious and crucial person, the editor, who will receive your book, and what happens once she has it? Will she just send it back unopened? Will she peek at it to be sure she is not missing a valuable book? How much will she read? Will she respond to you? How long will it take before she responds? If she thinks your book is publishable, how will you be informed?

In order to determine the current conditions of play, and to help finalize the recommendations on how to draft your proposal, I interviewed a representative number of editors. This chapter, in large part, is based on their responses.

In general, *most publishers accept unsolicited manuscripts*. Some editors who said they do not accept unsolicited manuscripts admit that when they receive one they take a peek; if the manuscript is intriguing, they will read the submission before they return it, and sometimes ask for more material. Almost all publishers will read a short query letter which identifies the subject and tone of the book you hope to submit.

Smaller publishers and university presses are generally the most receptive, and larger publishers the least receptive, to unsolicited manuscripts. Some publishers, such as those who publish romance novels and some publishers of children's books, look forward to receiving unsolicited manuscripts. *It is a myth that no publisher will accept unsolicited manuscripts.* Certainly, there are some major houses, inundated with author mail, that will only read agented manuscripts, but if you carefully select publishers and write to a specific editor, your manuscript can get in the front door of most publishing houses. Interesting sidelight: one of the largest and most prestigious trade publishers reported that all editorial assistants meet every three weeks and are treated to a pizza lunch as they read their way through unsolicited submissions. This is a tradition originated by the founders of the firm who, when they started, personally read every manuscript submitted.

The quantity of unsolicited manuscripts varies in direct proportion to the size of the publisher, and the estimates we received in the survey ranged from five to two hundred a week. One very successful midsized publisher, who said it was a tradition for him to read unsolicited manuscripts, commented that "every year the volume increases and the quality decreases." The problem for those authors who seek to be published is that there are thousands of other authors who do not make an effort to become skilled writers and salespersons, and their submissions may end up with yours. The challenge for you is to develop and exhibit your skill, talent, and professionalism in every way so you will be noticed and distinguished from the poorly prepared submissions.

The survey revealed that the person who reviews a manuscript is not always a low-level reader. In some houses, especially where the submission is directed to an editor by name, the editor herself reads the proposal (once again, the moral: write to the editor by name). In other instances and more commonly, it is an editorial assistant, a junior editor with limited experience, who is the reader. In a few instances, publishers use freelance readers. A most interesting finding was that in one small prestigious publishing house with respect for new talent, the editor-in-chief herself, whenever possible, looked through the unsolicited manuscripts. Many respondents reported that searching through the Slush Pile is like "looking for a needle in a haystack," but they still looked.

When we asked how much of the manuscript was read, the most frequent response was the first chapter or less. (Tip: get off to a fast and strong start.) Some said they read the first chapter and skim the rest; another respondent said she could tell the quality of the manuscript by reading the first ten pages. Some publishers said they read only the cover letter and the beginning and end of the manuscript. (Tip: keep it short.) Given the large influx of manuscripts and limited resources available, it is not surprising that very little of the manuscript is read. It is for this reason that one should *never submit a completed manuscript*, but send one or two sample chapters, along with a proposal, that will excite and intrigue a hurried and overworked reader.

Keep in mind that a fiction writer must have a finished novel before querying a publisher. Only veteran authors or those fortunate enough to write a highly successful first novel can sell their next work of fiction with just a summary or outline. With few exceptions, a novel must be complete; too many first-timers have started wonderfully but sputtered badly before finishing. You've got to prove you can finish the job, and that means a novel whose last page has been written.

The advantage of writing nonfiction, however, is that the book is rarely finished (most are barely begun) at the time of acquisition. The necessities of nonfiction writing are more easily identified; if a first-timer can write a smooth sample chapter, a convincing proposal, and a detailed chapter outline, the odds are that she can write the rest of the book in similar fashion. (Although one of the points of the proposal should be to convince the editor that the book is all but written.) As a matter of fact, I advise against finishing a work of nonfiction—unless it's something from the heart that you must write, why invest many months of your time in a book that may never be sold?

In general, the author is informed of a negative decision by a form letter. One publisher's form letter suggests that the author find an agent by consulting *LMP*. Some houses will modify the basic form letter; others have a variety of form letters. The turn-around time is generally from six to eight weeks. A few houses respond in a month, but the author should be prepared for a long wait for a response. Publishers understand that authors are likely to make multiple submissions, but they like to be informed if the manuscript is being sent to other publishers. Most publishers insist on a self-addressed stamped envelope (SASE) large enough to accommodate the manuscript; all publishers appreciate it. If the SASE is omitted, you risk not getting any response at all.

We asked respondents what happens when they read a manuscript that has merit. Some said they discussed the manuscript with others in the editorial department. After the discussion, they might write a letter with specific suggestions, and many said they would talk to the author on the telephone (so include your telephone number in your letter). In some instances, the reader would write a letter of general encouragement and ask to see more of your work, or if this was not a book in their area of interest, they would suggest other publishers who might be interested.

When we asked the editors what the chances were for a manuscript to move from the status of unsolicited manuscript to the point of serious consideration, the news was not very encouraging. The responses read:

- "once in a blue moon"
- "not very many make it"
- "accepted nothing in ten years" (another said nothing in twenty years)
- "small percentage"
- "2 out of 15 referred on, but they are ultimately rejected by the editor"
- "1 in a million" (another said 1 in 1000—that *is* better)
- "5 to 10 percent"
- "1 or 2 a year"

It is clear that the odds of the unsolicited manuscript moving to the stage where it will be read and possibly accepted are not great. Mostly this is due to the number of submissions received, the limited resources available to screen the manuscripts, and the poor quality of most submissions, which discourages some publishers from investing staff time in what they believe is an activity with a low return. If you are to beat these odds, you must use every skill at your command.

I asked the editors who reviewed unsolicited manuscripts for suggestions that could be passed on to you.

One editor suggested that you talk to an editor (who might be at a writers conference, for example) before starting the book and get advice as to the areas of interest of the publisher and the market served by the publisher. It would be fortuitous if the book you write fits into the publisher's "wish list." The same editor suggested a visit to bookstores to assess the market and avoid direct competition with well-established books (although there is almost always room for something better). Others suggested that you study publishers' lists to make sure the book you submit fits into their interests. These suggestions were repeated many times by other respondents.

Respondents repeatedly (and somewhat naively) suggested that the first-time author get an agent, especially for fiction. This was a common suggestion because, as an executive editor of a major publisher said, she expected the agent to "winnow" out the bad material. But many respondents went on to give helpful suggestions as to how to submit books directly to the publisher. The editors interviewed generally said they preferred a cover letter, a synopsis, a first and second chapter, and a bio. A query letter before submitting a proposal is useful, some said, especially for nonfiction.

When we asked the editors if they accept telephone calls, the responses were mixed. Some said "yes"; some said "no"; some said "no" with an exclamation mark—and others said "it depends." This is an area in which the first-time author should proceed with caution. A phone call is more appropriate if an author has received a letter with encouraging words from the editor.

Another editor suggested that the first-time author get feedback from someone other than a family member. Another said, "Do not make the package so difficult to open." One of the most dedicated of the editors in the business was a joy. She said she had been looking for nonfiction books about dogs (no wonder: *The Hidden Life of Dogs* by Elizabeth Marshall Thomas, published by Houghton Mifflin, was a big best-seller in 1993). And she also said, "It is *very* exciting to get a good unsolicited manuscript." With her dedication, it is no wonder that she discovered in the Slush Pile *Lily*, a western love story by Cindy Donner, which she published successfully, with an MGM film and a book sequel to come.

This was not the only success story that developed in the survey. *Thinkertoys*, a book about creativity in business by Michael Michalko, was an unsolicited manuscript, and became a major book, with foreign rights and book club sales. At another publishing house, *Car Pool*, a light, funny murder mystery by Mary Ghill, was discovered by an editorial assistant who subsequently worked closely with the author to make the book publishable. Not only was the author successfully published, but the editorial assistant, as a result of her work with the author, was promoted to associate editor. And still another publisher reported that *Sudie*, a novel by Sara Flanagan, was discovered in the Slush Pile and published successfully with paperback, TV movie, and foreign rights sales. These are just a few of the titles and authors discovered by publishers who regard reading unsolicited manuscripts a necessary part of their function.

While the odds of success are not great, the editors tell us that if the author has a quality book that is skillfully presented, it will rise up out of the Slush Pile to be recognized. One editor remarked that Judy Blume, the prolific teenage-fiction writer who broke new ground in the field, was discovered in the Slush Pile. The discovery of a best-selling author does not happen often, but if it happens just once, publishers are encouraged to accept and read unsolicited manuscripts. Your challenge is to make your submission so superior that it will set you apart from the "slush" in the Slush Pile. From that advice, we turn to the advice of an outstanding editor.

In a recent book, the question was asked: What makes an editor select a book? The question was satisfactorily answered by Richard Marek, the astute and respected editor with whom I had the good fortune to work for many years. When we worked together, he discovered Robert Ludlum, the best-selling author, and helped him become one of the most successful authors of spy fiction. In an essay which appears in Gerald Gross's book, *Editors on Editing*, Marek describes the editorial decision-making process. Marek says there are three kinds of books. First is the sales department book, which is more likely to be sought by the sales manager than the editor—"always nonfiction, fills a market need and is easily explained to the buyer."

The second kind, according the Marek, is the genre book: mysteries, romances, thrillers, "women's novels," gothics, histories. These are books that generate income from the sale of subsidiary rights. The reprint rights to these books are purchased by paperback houses and book clubs. (In view of today's market, where many of these categories go directly into paperback, this must be modified.)

The third category is the "editor's" book, which does not fall into any of the genres, but is acquired because of the author's "feel and passion." Such a book is *Jonathan Livingston Seagull*. Peter Mayer acquired the paperback rights when he was publisher at Avon Books for $1,000,000, and it was a huge success. Who, other than such a talented editor, would have thought an illustrated inspirational book about a seagull would sell millions of copies in paperback?

Today, in this multimedia world, editors, in selecting books, also look at the promotional possibilities of the book and the author. Is the author one who could do well on "Oprah" or "Donahue," TV shows that influence sales so strongly?

Marek says that, in reading a manuscript, he looks for something he has not seen before—a new idea, a new voice—"the jolt one feels at the unexpected." Books that epitomize this concept, Marek says, are *Moby Dick* by Herman Melville and the works of J. D. Salinger.

In fiction, Marek first looks for the voice. He asks himself, "Do I wish to spend the next several hours with the author? Do I trust him? Is he entertaining? Does he render familiar scenes in ways that are new, or unfamiliar ones in ways that make me see them clearly? Does he reveal enough of himself to make me like his company?"

After voice, there is pace. Is it a page-turner? In Ludlum, Marek explains, "Events move with the speed of a bullet."

Then there is character. "Do we *like* the characters? Do we care about their fates? Do we have an emotional investment in whether they marry or divorce, revenge themselves on those who did them wrong? Do they live? Are the complicated, surprising, *real*?" Marek says that if the answer is "yes" to these questions, the editor will be strongly influenced to buy the book.

Fourth is the plot. The story must draw us along because "we want to know what happens next, and whether what happens next convincingly surprises us. Arbitrary surprises won't do. Logical ones are glorious."

Next comes style. Marek says that "good writing is a lovely thing in and of itself, but it isn't enough to make me want to take on a book."

Finally, there is verisimilitude—not accuracy, but "if the author convinces me it's true, I don't care if it really is true or not."

For the first-time author of fiction, to meet these criteria is a major challenge, but it is what an editor seeks when she searches through the Slush Pile.

In nonfiction, the elements are the same but the priority is different. Marek puts voice first: "The reader must trust the author." The "hack" who presents his "groundbreaking" conclusion without logic is a loser.

As for subject matter, it might well be first instead. Subjects vary because tastes change. However, as reinforced by television fare, it seems "sex, money, murder, bizarre relationships, and the kinks of the rich and famous tend to be perennially popular." While Marek did not mention this, an excellent indicator of the perennially popular subject is *Reader's Digest*. Study several years of back issues, and the all-time favorite subjects of its readers are the nonfiction subjects listed on its covers.

Thirdly, Marek looks at the organization of material. "One wants to be led by an expert. The author sure of his facts, and selecting them wisely, is likely to convince us of his expertise."

There is also style. "The author who writes well can make even an unlikely subject seem interesting." John McPhee made Alaska fascinating, and more recently, Elizabeth Marshall Thomas made *The Hidden Life of Dogs* so accessible that it became a major best-seller.

Finally, as in fiction, there is verisimilitude. Marek writes, "Recently I read a book on something I really don't believe in: reincarnation. Yet the author made me believe that *he* believed and I read the book avidly, troubled and confused."

The technique of identifying a publisher and preparing an attractive proposal is not enough in itself. Richard Marek, speaking for all editors, has defined what editors look for in a manuscript. The quality of the writing must shine. Look to what you have written, listen to the voice, check the pace, live with the characters, review the plot (or in nonfiction, its credibility), study the style, and evaluate the verisimilitude. If you can find and rate these factors in your book on a scale of one to ten—and give yourself a seven to ten—you have a strong chance of attracting the editors who are anxious to find their next best-selling author.

6 The Book Proposal: Where the Author and Editor Meet

■ For thirty-four years, I read hundreds of book proposals, and in the last ten years, I have helped authors write them. The proposals are as varied as the personalities and subjects of the writers. But each successful one has the same qualities and components.

Established writers will submit a short summary of their book—sometimes as short as one $8\frac{1}{2}$ x 11-inch piece of paper—and have the book contract follow. Along with my editors, I have read a one-page story summary and, based on the author's reputation and previous books, authorized a million-dollar advance. The first-time writer does not have this luxury; she is unknown, without a track record, and unlikely to get a megabuck advance—and certainly not on a single-page outline. The techniques of writing a query letter or proposal are as different as the books presented in them. This chapter will address proposals. In the next chapter, you will find models that you should study and use to develop technique. But first the principle: the book proposal is designed to sell your book and *yourself*. The book proposal is an "interview" with the editor; it determines whether you get the opportunity you are seeking. So the proposal has to demonstrate your professionalism and your ability to write. A well-written proposal says you can write a publishable book.

Despite the differences in books, there are some general rules that apply for all book proposals, and because they are so basic, they are discussed first. In her article "What Editors Look For" in Gerald Gross's *Editors on Editing*, Jane von Mehren begins her advice on writing a proposal with these rules. I agree with hers, and have added some of my own.

The Basics

The Format

1. Letters and all enclosures should be typed. In these days of computers, you have a choice of typefaces. Select a common, readable typeface (at least 10-point, preferably 12-point), then make certain your printer is operating on its best behavior, so the material you submit is dark enough, attractive, and readable. Always use black ink, and never use a dot-matrix printer—letter-quality is best.

2. Use uniform $8^1/_2$ x 11-inch paper, preferably a good white bond paper. Use normal margins, usually $1^1/_2$ inches on the top and to the left, and 1 inch to the right and on the bottom.

3. Always double-space the summary, or table of contents, and sample chapter. The cover letter and bio can be single-spaced.

4. Identify each part of your proposal by starting a new sheet (e.g., Summary, Table of Contents, Sample Chapter, Bio). Number all pages so that it is easy for the reader to follow.

5. Check spelling and grammar and proofread everything in your proposal. A sloppy manuscript is a turnoff.

6. Avoid fancy headlines or use of exotic type. The proposal should be neat, dignified, and inviting to read.

7. As I've said before, address your submission to a specific person determined by your research.

8. Keep a copy of what you send, including your cover letter.

9. Enclosed a self-addressed, stamped envelope (SASE) or mailer if you want your manuscript returned.

10. Always include your name, address, telephone number, and where applicable, fax number.

Once you've cover the basics, determine your strategy. If you are out to locate potential buyers and your subject, usually nonfiction, can be explained in a letter, you might use a query letter to do this.

The Query Letter

The query letter is a pithy, enticing letter from the author to the editor which encourages the editor to ask for more. This technique is used extensively in seeking magazine assignments, where most assignments are for nonfiction articles and where the content can be described readily in a letter of one to two pages (but not much longer). Yours should ideally run one page, get to the point quickly, and persuade the editor to ask to see the rest of your material.

Some book editors in our survey suggested that first-time authors use query letters because it gives the editor a way to respond more quickly and more directly to the book idea presented. My recommendation to first-time authors is: use a query letter only for nonfiction. A short, dramatic presentation of a nonfiction concept encourages an editor to ask for a full proposal. The best positive response to a query letter is a request for the author to send in a proposal. The author should have a full-fledged proposal ready to send to an editor who expresses interest in the project. A long hiatus between an expression of interest in response to a query letter and the submission of a proposal might well be counterproductive.

The Book Proposal

The book proposal, especially for a work of nonfiction, is the preferred method of getting an editor's attention. The function of the book proposal is to so excite the editor who reads it that she will write, telephone, or fax the author, inviting a discussion which will lead to a contract to publish the book. *Never submit a complete manuscript.* (The only exception to this would be for a juvenile picture book or novel, when the entire story is relatively short.) On the other hand, if you send only a few assorted pages of the manuscript without a summary of the book or information about you, the editor will not understand what she is reading, what your book is saying, or who you are. You have minutes, not hours, of the editor's attention, so use this time judiciously. Create a proposal with four, possibly five, parts to it.

1. The Cover Letter—This, much like a query letter, must:

- make an impact;
- describe the book, including the permissions, illustrations, and photographs needed, and who will provide them;
- define the market;
- evaluate the competition—show how and why your book is either newer, better, needed, more comprehensive—or all of these and more;
- set out the scope of content;
- show why you are the perfect person to write the book;
- estimate the length;
- tell when the book could be completed.

The cover letter must have impact, compelling the editor to read on. Remember, editors are very busy, and are just looking for an excuse to toss your letter aside. Don't give them one.

2. Summary—Having been attracted by your cover letter, the summary of the book should draw the editor further into your book proposal. The summary, depending on the complexity, can be from one to ten pages in length, and sets out clearly and in reasonable detail just what the book is about. A good summary, or overview, of a nonfiction book vividly and quickly introduces the book's concept; makes clear the style in which it will be written; shows how and why there is a need for it; defines the book's audience as specifically as possible, both quantitatively and qualitatively; and details its competition, showing how this book is different and better in some way. For a work of fiction, the proposal can be shorter and simpler, merely describing your novel and giving a short summary of its contents.

3. The Sample Chapter(s)—While the summary is a quick synopsis of the book that illustrates your writing skill, the sample chapter(s) should introduce the editor to the essence of your book and your writing style, and make the editor wish she had the rest of the book to read. Most editors want to see the first chapter and possibly a second chapter. Provide only enough *high-quality* material to show the promise of your book.

4. Table of Contents—Since the sample chapter is only a sample of the book, you should furnish a table of contents for your planned nonfiction book. This is absolutely essential. It demonstrates the scope of the book, and the logic you use in presenting the information to the reader. In many instances, a detailed chapter breakdown, with one or two paragraphs about the material to be covered in each chapter, is helpful. It shows the editor that you know how to organize the material and that there is enough material to make a book (see pages 69–73 for an example of an expanded table of contents).

5. The Bio—If the editor is satisfied with the summary and the sample chapter, the bio should reassure the editor who asks: Can this author really complete this book? Does she have the background or credentials to write a successful book? The editor has heard of untutored, first-time authors who are successful (such as Margaret Mitchell who only wrote one book, *Gone with the Wind*, which became a best-selling book, won a Pulitzer Prize, and later became the basis for an enduring film), but she is wary. You are an unknown. She needs the comfort of knowing you have life experiences that support the positive feelings she has developed after reading the cover letter, the summary, the sample chapter, and the table of contents. You must assure her that you are the right person to write this book. Anything indicating professional writing experience, or expertise in the subject of your book, should be included.

The author should also describe what she can do to promote the book: contacts with organizations, the media, and colleagues, for instance. Include any media and public speaking experience. If this is lengthy, it may be a section of its own. Publishers love authors who understand the limitations of marketing budgets and who are fully prepared to assist actively in the publicity and promotion of their book. If you propose to promote and demonstrate the book by making personal appearances (for example, for an exercise book), enclose a photograph.

6. What Not to Include—For a children's book that you will write but not illustrate, do not include any illustrations. (If your book is accepted the publisher will find an illustrator for it.) Do not burden your presentation with any other material. The sparse, well-organized presentation is more likely to be read and lead to a request for more material. Send in the entire manuscript only if the text of your children's book or poetry book is just a few pages.

7. Pulling It All Together—To organize these elements in your mind and settle on what to include in your book proposal, visualize a group of young editors sitting around a table eating pizza (a real-life situation), and visualize one editor reaching for your proposal. In your mind's eye, look over her shoulder as she selects your package.

First, she will read your captivating cover letter (one page, two at the most). Second, she will read your excellent summary of the book and be so taken with it that she will wish to read … (third) your table of contents (nonfiction only). Fourth, she will read your sample chapter (or put it in her carry-home bag to read at home) along with your bio, and soon will write or call you with good news.

8. Do's and Don'ts—Here are some suggestions that will increase your chances of success.

- *Don't* send in an entire manuscript. Editors have reported that they read only the first ten pages at most. You are better served with a sample chapter.
- *Do* work hard in selecting a title that is a "stopper." A catchy title that succinctly and memorably communicates what your book is about is ideal. If you cannot come up with one, identify your title as a tentative or working title.
- *Don't* try to be an amateur marketer of your book. Let experienced salespeople develop the "selling handle" to be used in presenting the book to a book buyer. You can and should *suggest* how to reach and appeal to your book's market.
- *Do* let others, especially people in the publishing industry, read your proposal. Listen to their suggestions, but accept only those with which you are comfortable.
- *Do* make sure you have appropriate, written permission for the use of material from other books or the names of individuals you are including in your book.
- *Do* look at competitive books if yours is nonfiction, and *do* compare your book realistically (and let's hope, favorably) with those books in your cover letter. If you have or can get the published sales figures for competitive books, *do* include this information as well.
- *Do* follow up after about sixty days, knowing that reading unsolicited manuscripts is a low priority. Try a follow-up letter first and then a telephone call to the assistant to the editor to whom you wrote.

9. Why This Method Words—Obviously, no one can guarantee that any book proposal system will result in the acceptance of a manuscript. Even experienced literary agents with excellent contacts can't guarantee that a writer's work will be accepted. This method, however, helps you establish relationships with editors, and a good relationship between an editor and an author is precious.

The editor is in publishing because she delights in finding good books and talented authors, and in seeing her books appear on a publishing list. Aside from the reality that most publishing houses are deluged with manuscripts and never provide sufficient staff to review the Slush Pile, editors prefer to see a book at its earliest stage and prefer a submission by a first-time author in a proposal form. Using a proposal, an editor can evaluate the concept of the book, review the table of contents, read the sample chapter, and then make a meaningful, creative contribution to the book as she shapes it for publication. To discover work from a new author is the dream of every editor. She needs you and you need her. Professionalism on your part can help make this relationship happen.

If you have chosen an attractive book concept, developed it with skill, carefully selected the publishers to whom you submit the work, identified the appropriate editors, prepared the book proposal artfully, and are determined and persistent, you will increase the chances that your book captures the attention of a publisher.

In the following chapter, you will find samples of a query letter, cover letter, summary, sample chapter, biography, and finally a complete proposal. In some instances, I drafted these myself. In other instances, I selected outstanding models submitted by my clients, actual aspiring writers. The models are at a level of excellence you can achieve or exceed. Review these samples carefully and compare them to the quality of what you submit. Make every part of your proposal the best it can be. The competition to get published, both from first-time authors and established writers alike is fierce. To win, you must use every advantage available.

7 Models—Query Letter, Cover Letter, Summary, Sample Chapter, and Bio

■ The dual role of an author and agent requires you to be self-critical. To help you, I have selected and, in some instances where material was not available, created models of the components of the proposal: a query letter, a cover letter, a summary, a sample chapter, a table of contents (and some variations on the theme), and a bio. Together, these elements should combine to form a persuasive, compelling proposal.

These models and the comments that precede them will help you create and check the quality of your submission. Since your book will be different from the books used in the models, these samples will serve as idea generators and illustrate a level of quality and a format that you can apply to your own proposal.

You will find on the following pages:

■ **Query Letter**—a letter used primarily when publishers do not accept unsolicited manuscripts or when you wish to determine interest from a wide range of potential publishers. Models are for nonfiction and fiction.

■ **Cover Letter**—a letter that accompanies and introduces a full-scale proposal, including a summary, a table of contents, sample chapter, and a bio. Models are for nonfiction and fiction.

■ **Summary**—a condensation of the information in the book. The model is for nonfiction, which also addresses the market and the competition; a longer summary than appears in the cover letter is not necessary for a fiction proposal—better to send an actual sample.

■ **Table of Contents**—a list of the contents by chapter indicating the scope and organization of the book. Models are for nonfiction only and include an expanded version that combine a summary with table of contents.

■ **Sample Chapter(s)**—one or two chapters that indicate the author's style, voice, and quality of writing. Samples are provided for nonfiction and fiction.

■ **Bio**—the author's resumé illustrating the background she brings to the work. Models are presented in resumé form and in paragraph form.

The material is this chapter illustrates each component of an effective proposal, one that is likely to attract the attention of the editor reading unsolicited manuscripts. The material written especially for this chapter is of a level that you can achieve. When you complete your proposal, ask yourself the question, "Does my proposal read as well as the models?" If the answer is "yes," your proposal meets the test.

Query Letter

Nonfiction

A good query letter meets the standards listed below. The following sample covers all these bases in one short page, thereby increasing the likelihood that it will be read and that it will get a positive response.

- addressed to a specific editor
- conveys the scope and tone of the book

- short and to the point
- uses anecdotes to intrigue the editor
- identifies the size of the potential market
- discusses the competition
- estimates the length of the book
- encourages the editor to ask for the full proposal
- encloses a bio
- encloses a self-addressed, stamped envelope

■

Sample Nonfiction Query Letter*

August 16, 1995

Ms. Mary K. Smith
Editor
H&W Publishing
200 Avenue B
Somewhere, PA 11002

Dear Mary K. Smith:

I am an anthropologist and I have always lived with dogs, and I believe behind the wet nose and the wagging tail there is a hidden life.

In my book, which I plan to call *The Hidden Life of Dogs*, I will tell about the eleven dogs with whom I have lived.

In my book readers will meet Misha, a husky who jumped a fence daily and roamed a suburban territory of 160 square miles, and Mara, his true love, who bore his first puppies and then, after he moved away with new owners, gave herself indifferently to any adequate male passerby.

This will be a book about dog consciousness. Humans are not the only beings who have thoughts or emotions. Dogs have thoughts and feelings, they adopt human mannerisms, they make choices, they smile.

The book, although not scientific in nature, will report on what I

---

* This is not a real query letter, but one I created as an illustration, using a published book. I am sure that Elizabeth Marshall Thomas could have written a better query letter—as you may know, her book *The Hidden Life of Dogs*, published by Houghton Mifflin, was a #1 best-seller in 1993 and will continue to sell for many, many years.

estimate to be 100,000 hours of observation. This will be a popular book for the millions of dog owners who know that their dog has a hidden life which they wish to understand. As far as I can find, there is no competitive book on the market.

I visualize this as a book of about 144 pages, which I can complete in about one year.

I hope you are sufficiently interested to respond to me so I can send you the table of contents and the first chapter. My bio is enclosed and on it you will find my address, telephone, and fax numbers.

Sincerely,

Elizabeth Marshall Thomas

Enclosure (Bio, SASE)

Fiction

The sample fiction query letter is written to a specialized publisher—in this instance, one that publishes romance books. The writer tells enough of the story to interest the editor and explain why she is uniquely qualified to write this book. She has asked for an answer and provided the essential information for a response. The letter meets the following standards:

- addressed to a specific editor
- identifies the topic of romance
- has an intriguing twist—the Russian locale, which has rarely been written about before
- tells the story in a high-concept form
- sets the estimated length
- states how long it would take to write
- gives the editor the "inspirational ending" of the novel
- establishes the author's qualifications to write the book
- short and to the point

■

Sample Fiction Query Letter

Croydon Towers
33 Bleecker Street
New York, NY 10013
Phone: 212-555-1234
Fax: 212-555-4321

September 9, 1994

Ms. Millicent Middlemarch
Editor, Romance Line
Pinnacle Books
1234 S. 21st Street
Philadelphia, PA 23456

Dear Ms. Middlemarch:

Romance abounds in the area of the world that formerly lay behind the Iron Curtain, yet this is undiscovered territory for the romance novel today. I have a file of romance story ideas of loving relationships that were threatened by the harshness of life in these countries. I am preparing to write a series of romance novels utilizing this material.

My first book, *Gorky Street*, which will be about 75,000 words in length, is set in Russia. The heroine is Yulia, the daughter of a famous Russian general, who is forced into a loveless marriage with a KGB official. On a trip to the United States with her father, Yulia, who acts as his English interpreter, falls in love with an American diplomat. Yulia realizes that she must not in any way encourage this relationship.

With the downfall of the Communist Party, her husband and father are stripped of their ranks and benefits. Yulia, because of her English language skills, is sought out and becomes the editor of a popular English-language magazine. She provides the main source of income for her proud father and husband. Yulia learns that she obtained the job because of the American diplomat, who fell in love with her when she was in the United States. He comes to Russia to urge her to leave the hardships and disarray of her native land, divorce her husband, and become his wife.

The chance to go to the United States, to live comfortably, to get out from under the tight control of her father and husband, and to raise a family, is attractive. Yulia agrees to leave and then is tormented by her decision. She elects to stay, make her own country better, be loyal to her father, and build a future with her husband.

Having lived in Moscow with my husband, who was a correspondent for the *New York Times* for three years, I have the background needed to write this story. As you will see in my bio, I have written nonfiction extensively for magazines. I should be able to complete this in a year.

I hope this concept for a novel will interest you so that I may send you a full proposal.

Sincerely,

Jennifer Jordan

Enclosure (Bio, SASE)

Cover Letter

Nonfiction

The cover letter introduces the editor to the book proposal. This sample for nonfiction contains the following elements:

- catchy opening paragraph that presents the "high concept"
- a second paragraph that opens the door to the book by identifying some of the specifics to be included
- a description of the "voice" to be used (e.g., nontechnical)
- the length of the book
- a description of the enclosures in the proposal
- the omnipresent SASE

■

Sample Cover Letter for Nonfiction*

July 19, 1994

Ms. Mary K. Wang
Editor
Wang & Hill
19 Union Square West
New York, NY 10019

Dear Ms. Wang:

Recent studies have found that one woman in five, and one man in ten, will suffer from depression some time during the course of their lives. This is a disturbing statistic but there is hope, because more and more evidence has surfaced to indicate that many psychiatric disorders are chemical imbalances that can be successfully treated with medication.

Our book, *Understanding Depression*, will be a definitive guide to depressive illness—its causes, course, and signposts, written in terms the lay reader can understand. We will include several self-rating tests in the book enabling the reader to determine whether or not he should seek psychiatric evaluation. We will describe the symptoms of chemical depression (as opposed to nonchemical depression—a more common illness).

The book will be written in human terms and in reader-friendly language, and we will use excerpts from patient histories to show the progress of typical patients and their recovery.

We will discuss the various antidepression medications (including Prozac), and the benefits and side effects of these drugs. This will be a readable guide to this much misunderstood illness. As you are aware, there have been a number of books on the drugs and the illness. Our book will be the most comprehensive book available.

We believe the book will be about 50,000 to 75,000 words and will be completed six months after we get a positive answer from you.

We have included a table of contents, the introduction to the book, and Chapter 1, which we feel is a good sample of our writing style.

---

*I wrote this letter as a hypothetical illustration from the material found in *Understanding Depression*, by Donald F. Klein, M.D. and Paul H. Wender, M.D., published by Oxford University Press, 1993.

Our curricula vitae are included, which will provide you with addresses and telephone numbers at which you can reach us. A self-addressed, stamped envelope is also enclosed.

We look forward to your response.

Donald F. Klein, M.D.

Paul H. Wender, M.D.

Fiction

The sample cover letter for fiction has been based on a sequel to the famous Arthur C. Clarke novel, *2001: A Space Odyssey.* This illustration demonstrates an effective but brief cover letter and covers the following bases. If the cover letter encourages the editor to read further, it has accomplished its purpose.

- sets up the premise of the book in "high-concept" style in the first two paragraphs to engage the editor's interest
- provides a title that describes the book
- identifies the enclosures
- explains that this is a multiple submission—with a preference for the publisher to whom it is being submitted

■

Sample Cover Letter for Fiction*

Astro House
12 Round Hill Road
Dallas, TX 87674
Telephone: 405-555-7788
Fax: 405-555-8877

Ms. Mary K. Wright
Up and Down Publishing
10 Harbor Drive
Port Chester, NY 10581

Dear Ms. Wright:

My novel is set in the first year of the twenty-second century, the year 2101. The commander of *Discovery*, a spacecraft traveling at a hundred thousand miles an hour, is closing in on its destination, the farthest edge of the solar system. The crew includes a navigator, three deep-freeze hypernauts, and Hal, a chatty computer who guides them.

The mission was set off by a shrinking slab found within the moon's crater Clavius. This is a deliberately buried calling card left by an alien intelligence millions of years ago. And the crew must find answers wherever and whatever they are.

My working title for the novel is *2101: Second Space Odyssey*. I expect it to run between 75,000 and 100,000 words and take about a year to complete.

I am enclosing a plot summary, table of contents, a sample chapter, and an informal bio. Please read on—and call or fax me or write to me at the address shown above. I have enclosed a self-addressed, stamped envelope.

Sincerely,

Arthur C. Clarke

P.S.: This is a multiple submission; however, I sense a good fit with Up and Down's science fiction list and am especially interested in your reaction to this proposal.

---

* This description was adapted from the copy contained in the paperback version of Arthur C. Clarke's best-seller, *2001: A Space Odyssey*, published by Signet Books of New American Library, which has sold over three million copies.

Summary

Nonfiction

Two crucial parts of the proposal are the summary, or overview, and the sample chapter, preferably the first chapter of the book. A good summary encourages the editor to read the sample chapter. The summary should convey enough about the book to give the editor reading it reason to believe there is enough material for a successful book. Demonstrating the scope and thrust of the book and assuring the editor that the author can write effectively are the primary purposes of the summary. It should also, however, address the market for the book, its competition, and why the book is superior in some way. The sample summary shown for nonfiction is the actual summary submitted by Professor Gerald Gunther, whom I represented, which resulted in the sale of his book, a biography of Learned Hand.

Although Professor Gunther, a constitutional law scholar, had written the best-selling case book used in constitutional law classes, this was his first trade book and his first major biography. He had access to thousands of letters, memos, and legal opinions that were made available to him in order to write the book, but it was necessary that his summary demonstrate his ability to write an engaging biography.

In his opening paragraph, the author established the major premise of his book: the life of jurist Learned Hand. It was necessary, in the beginning, to assure the publisher that this book was not to be a recital of the cases decided by a famous judge, but a personal saga. The author described in detail the sources he was using, including his personal observations as a clerk to Judge Hand.

This exceptional example of a summary for a nonfiction book sets forth the subject, the material, and the author's point of view, and demonstrates the author's ability to write for a general audience. Also touched upon are the market (audience) for the book, and the book's competition (or lack of it).

■

Sample Nonfiction Summary

LEARNED HAND: THE MAN AND THE JUDGE
(working title)

By Gerald Gunther
William Nelson Cromwell Professor of Law
Stanford Law School

The major purpose of the biography is to explore the distinctive ingredients of the public figure and of the private man; and my central objective is to delineate the interdependence of the public and the private in Learned Hand.

Hand's public career prompts my biography, but it is by no means its exclusive concern. The career was impressive. Although he never sat on the Supreme Court, Hand (1872-1961) was a federal judge for over 50 years, and he is widely regarded as ranking with Holmes and Brandeis and Cardozo in 20th-century American judging. Moreover, his public life was intertwined with some of the main strands of 20th-century political and intellectual developments. For example, in the first decade of the century, he was one of that small group of New York City intellectuals presiding over the birth of the *New Republic* magazine; he was an advisor to Theodore Roosevelt in the Progressive movement and indeed ran for public office on the Bull Moose ticket soon after he became a federal judge; and even after his withdrawal from partisan activities after World War I, he maintained close ties (and sustained an extensive correspondence) with figures ranging from Bernard Berenson to Walter Lippmann, Felix Frankfurter, and J. D. Salinger.

But my interest in Hand goes substantially beyond those ingredients of the public image. I am especially intrigued by the complex interrelationship between the private man and the public figure. In Hand's case, there is a wealth of information. Most important is the collection of Learned Hand Papers, a collection of about one hundred thousand items, to which I have exclusive access. (The Papers were given to Harvard Law School on the condition that they remain closed until the biography is done. I am the designated biographer; and the major portions of the Papers are in my possession.) I know of no papers on the 20th century comparable to these in depth, range, and candor. Hand did not like the telephone or dictating to a stenographer; he was more like a 19th- than a 20th-century correspondent in finding it most congenial to record his deepest thoughts via pen and ink and, unlike a John Quincy Adams or a Felix Frankfurter, he did so without any self-conscious sense of history looking over his shoulder.

Hand was an unusually introspective as well as articulate individual, and his correspondence is filled with his reflections not only on the world around him, about political and philosophical and literary and legal issues, but about himself as well. Moreover, I came to know Learned Hand and to spend many hours with him in his last years, after serving as his law clerk in 1953-54. Beyond that, I have interviewed many persons who knew him well.

The special importance of Learned Hand, the public man, lies in the way he executed the task of judging and of dealing with the controversies of a long, tumultuous period in American history. Two models of judging have competed in the endless search for the proper role of the judiciary in our constitutional democracy. One model, the interventionist, activist one, is evaluated (and often admired) largely in terms of the ends it seeks—"justice," "equality," etc. Earl Warren and William O. Douglas are among the major modern illustrations of that model. Learned Hand is the best example of the competing, more modest and restrained yet also creative model, a model which assesses judges more in terms of process rather than results. That modest model places the highest value on open-mindedness, detachment, and impartiality in approach, on thorough analysis, and on persuasiveness in reasoning.

I believe that Hand's judicial career is the single strongest datum we have to demonstrate that the modest yet creative model of judging is attainable. Not only does Hand rank with Holmes and Frankfurter as a leading articulator of that model, but his performance on the lower federal courts, more clearly than that of any Supreme Court Justice, illustrates that the model is achievable in real life. To a remarkable degree, Learned Hand managed to behave as the modest judge should.

How did Hand manage it? What accounts for his rare capacity to practice what so many others, not only Hand, have preached? What kind of person could achieve such a rare congruence of theory and practice in judging? Pursuit of these questions is the major aim of my book. Hand's judicial career provides the impetus for examining his life. But a judicial biography, certainly Hand's, must go beyond. Accordingly, a central focus of my study is the human being beneath the judicial robes. That emphasis discloses numerous clues to an understanding of the complex personality that made possible, and perhaps compelled, the performance of the judicial task in Hand's way.

While most sketches of Hand depict him as a magisterial, serene figure, Learned Hand viewed himself as driven by self-doubts and uncer-
tainty for most of his nine decades. Outside observers and the subject
himself seemingly produced contradictory portraits. Yet there are elements of truth in each: the preeminent judge was a product of the driven, self-doubting man, long before he became a judge. Reflectiveness,
questioning, skepticism, intolerance of absolutes, a relentless search for
answers despite an abiding conviction that there were no permanent
ones: these traits emerged gradually in his Albany youth, matured at
Harvard, and were cemented in his few years of law practice before
ascending the bench. And, most impressively, Hand did not stop doubting, searching, and growing during his long judicial career.

Throughout Hand's life, his reflectiveness and skepticism were entan-
gled with the darker, "can't help" elements of indecisiveness and melan-
choly. Throughout an increasingly distinguished career, he never ceased
doubting the worth of his own work and the justifiability of the mount-
ing applause. The self-doubt permeated all aspects of his life: there was
recurrent self-questioning and moodiness and gloom. Yet these dark
agonies did not produce intellectual paralysis.

One of the few issues on which Hand held strong convictions was the
choice between the models of judging. He believed that the modest,
restrained, disinterested role was the only proper one for a judge in a
democratic society. It was a conviction nurtured by the teaching of
James Bradley Thayer at Harvard Law School and by the abuses of judicial power during the Lochner era in the early decades of the 20th century. Hand's unmatched capacity to behave in practice in accordance
with the prescriptions of the modest model was in part a rational, logical deduction from theoretical premises. But in at least equal part, it was
a product of sensitivity, wisdom and, above all, another "can't help": the
skeptical, doubting, open-minded human being could not help acting
that way as a judge.

I view myself as writing for a general audience rather than a predom-
inantly legal one, and I therefore do not plan to discuss his more than
three thousand judicial opinions in detail. Rather, I illustrate his manner of
deciding cases through a discussion of a number of illustrative clusters,
relying on his revealing letters as well as his published and unpublished
opinions. In selecting the illustrative areas, I expect to use those of
greatest interest, especially those on constitutional questions. Opinions
on freedom of political speech, obscenity, copyright, and deportation for
lack of "good moral character" are my prime candidates for these discussions. My major concern will be to delineate how Hand's personality

and character shaped his public career and his concept of the judicial role. In my discussion of the judicial career, I will emphasize his temper and character (and his political and intellectual environment) rather than the details of legal rules. In this manner, I expect to cast important new light on the judicial philosophy reflected in the frequently reprinted collection of his papers and addresses, *The Spirit of Liberty* (1952) and his Holmes Lectures, *The Bill of Rights* (1958).

I do not believe that there is much need to explicate the contemporary relevance of Learned Hand and his career. The competing models of American constitutional judging—the model of the modest, restrained judge as against that of the activist, interventionist one— stirred debate even during the era of the Framers. That debate pervades our history. The controversy continues today, and will tomorrow. Learned Hand's career is widely considered to be the best modern example of the modest yet creative model, and it is that role of Hand's that largely prompted me to undertake this biography.

Nor do I need to belabor the relevance to humanistic interests of a broad-gauged biography of one of the greatest of America's judges. But the ties between Hand and the humanities go beyond my general theme. For example, at Harvard College in the early 1890s, Hand's major teachers were Josiah Royce and William James and George Santayana, during the Golden Age of Harvard's Philosophy Department. Had it not been for family pressure to join the legal profession, Hand would no doubt have pursued graduate work in philosophy. Beyond that, Hand's life and work constitute an outstanding example of the humanities-oriented judge. I cannot resist concluding with a well-known, especially apt passage from Hand's writings:

> I venture to believe that it is important to a judge called upon to pass upon a question of constitutional law, to have at least a bowing acquaintance with Acton and Maitland, with Thucydides, Gibbon and Carlyle, with Homer, Dante, Shakespeare and Machiavelli, Montaigne and Rabelais, with Plato, Bacon, Hume and Kant, as with the books which have been specifically written on the subject. For in such matters everything turns upon the spirit in which he approaches the questions before him... Men do not gather figs off thistles, nor supply institutions from judges whose outlook is limited.

That passage captures a theme at the very core of Hand; its substance echoes throughout his letters and his life.

The Table of Contents

Including a table of contents is only necessary, or advisable, in a nonfiction proposal. The purpose of the table of contents is to show the scope of the book, and that the remainder of the book beyond the sample chapter has been well thought out. If the chapter headings are indicative of the content, the editor can visualize how the book will develop.

Lee Iacocca, legendary for rebuilding Chrysler Motors after having been fired from Ford Motor Company after thirty-two years of service, regularly had his hair cut by the same barber at the Waldorf-Astoria in New York. In 1983, so the story goes, the editor-in-chief of Bantam Books, who also used this barber, asked him to arrange an introduction to Lee Iacocca. The book developed out of this meeting was *Iacocca*, and it became a breakthrough book with multi-million-copy sales in hardcover, and then a multi-million-copy paperback. (An interesting note is that the barber sued Bantam for an agent's commission, and the case was settled out of court.)

The table of contents in *Iacocca* is an excellent model because of its depth and organization. It is possible to see the four sections of the book, the chronology of the story, and the author's advice which concludes the book. The scope, depth, and pace of the book is set forth on this one-page table of contents. It does not get much better, or simpler, than this.

■

Sample Nonfiction Table of Contents

CONTENTS

Acknowledgments ix
An Opening Word xi
Prologue xii

MADE IN AMERICA

I   The Family 3
II   School Days 13

THE FORD STORY

III   Getting My Feet Wet 29
IV   The Bean Counters 38
V   The Key to Management 46
VI   The Mustang 61
VII   Encore! 78
VIII   The Road to the Top 86
IX   Trouble in Paradise 98
X   1975: The Fateful Year 111
XI   The Showdown 120
XII   The Day After 133

THE CHRYSLER STORY

XIII   Courted by Chrysler 141
XIV   Aboard a Sinking Ship 151
XV   Building the Team 167
XVI   The Day the Shah Left Town 182
XVII   Drastic Measures: Going to the Government 192
XVIII Should Chrysler Be Saved? 202
XIX   Chrysler Goes to Congress 213
XX   Equality of Sacrifice 229
XXI   The Banks: Trial by Fire 239
XXII   The K-Car—And a Close Call 251
XXIII Public Man, Public Office 267
XXIV   A Bittersweet Victory 278

STRAIGHT TALK

XXV   How to Save Lives on the Road 293
XXVI   The High Cost of Labor 303
XXVII The Japanese Challenge 314
XXVIII Making America Great Again 324

       Epilogue: The Great Lady 339
       Index 343

■

Expanded Table of Contents

In some instances, the table of contents for a nonfiction book can be expanded to form a detailed chapter outline. If your subject lends itself to this type of treatment, use this model as an idea generator.

The editor receiving an expanded table of contents can tell by reading a few pages what the book will include, the tone of the book, the pace, and can anticipate the reader's interest in the subject. She will be impressed by your detailed preparation and thoughtful organization. Many experienced editors find a description of what will appear in each chapter far preferable to a "naked" table of contents.

Following is an example of an expanded tables of contents for a nonfiction book, *The Business of Publishing*, created by the author to illustrate this technique.

■

Sample Nonfiction Expanded Table of Contents

THE BUSINESS OF PUBLISHING

PART I — THE EDITORIAL PROCESS

Chapter I. From the Idea to the Creation of the Business

The business of publishing begins with the editorial decision. If it is a start-up business, this is the most crucial of all decisions. What does the author offer the consumer that is unique or, if not unique, published better than ever before? S&S started with a line of crossword puzzle books. Harry Abrams, the distinguished art book publisher, started with a line of books, "The Library of Great Painters." Random House started with Modern Library. Each of these publishing stories will be told dramatically.

Chapter II. How Editorial Decisions Make Businesses Grow

Often, the editorial decisions are more narrowly focused. In some instances, it is a decision as to whether or not to start or add a line (stories of how *The How and Why Books* were started, and how John Muir moved into juvenile publishing when the travel book business was adversely affected by the recession in travel). But still, it is a decision that is made on a title-by-title basis.

Chapter III. The Sources for Books

Where do books come from? From agents, from packagers, from direct solicitation of an author (finding an article in a magazine written by an author you wish to develop), and from the unsolicited manuscript. The most creative form of editorial development is to bring an idea and author together and work to develop both. Or to be able to recognize the talent in an author that can be developed in another genre (Erica Jong from poet to novelist). Or to find a book that, with editing, can be made into a best-seller (story of Don Fine converting *Storm Island* into *Eye of the Needle*). One final, more difficult source, unless you are well-qualified, is foreign translation (story of Arcade).

Chapter IV. How Editorial Departments Are Organized

Organization chart of the Editorial Department. The functions to be performed are merged in smaller organizations and done by fewer people (story of a $5-million art book company staffed by three full-time people, with all the rest working on a freelance basis).

Chapter V. The Editorial Process

The process: the book is read by the acquiring editor, informal conference or short write-up for editor-in-chief, the first decision to accept or reject, the editorial conference, the acceptance or rejection, the negotiation of terms, and the referral to contract department.

Chapter VI. Making the Editorial Decision

Using financial and market analysis forms, explain how input is collected from marketing, production, and advertising departments, and how proposal is made to the editorial committee. In a smaller firm, these functions are performed by contacting salesmen or key customers, using a printer or production consultant, etc. Explain and illustrate how pricing and format (hardcover vs. softcover) decisions are made.

If the editorial process ends here, prepare for disaster. The most important part of the process is the post mortem. One year after publication, review the economic projections vs. reality. Learn from your successes and from your failures.

PART II — PRODUCTION

Chapter VII. The Production Process

The editorial department transmits the manuscript to the production department. The first port of call is copyediting (often done outside the company), and then the manuscript goes to the art department for interior design and cover design. (This section will be illustrated to show copyedited manuscript as well as interior and cover designs, illustrating the pitfalls and the winning techniques.) There will also be a discussion of desktop publishing.

Chapter VIII. The Printing Process

A short primer on the various forms of printing with both domestic and foreign sources described with tips on when to use a domestic source and when to go abroad.

PART III — MARKETING

Chapter IX. Making Marketing Decisions

How the basic marketing decisions are made. How the marketing department is involved in the production and editorial decisions (for instance, pricing, bulk of books, title, copy lines, reviewer quotes on the jacket, etc.) when the book is acquired. The "team" approach to publishing.

Chapter X. The Many Markets for Books

Each area of selling the book is examined: independent trade, chain stores, superstores, wholesalers, special sales, foreign sales. Starts with the organization of the marketing department and follows through with who does what and why.

Chapter XI. Book Advertising

The role of advertising as related to the realities of how much a publisher can spend and where to spend it (author tours, print space, radio, TV, etc.). Illustrated with a typical campaign.

Chapter XII. The New Developments in Marketing

The new developments in the mass market, super wholesalers such as Sams, Advanced Marketing, etc. will be discussed along with more traditional areas of the bargain book and remainder markets, book clubs, and direct mail.

Chapter XIII. Book Fairs

A section on the show to attend (for example, Frankfurt, ABA, London Book Fair, Bologna, etc.). The value of the Fairs and how to get maximum benefit.

PART IV — Financial

Chapter XIV. The Role of the Financial Officer

The role of the financial officer in publishing, illustrating how the finance department is involved in the editorial, production, and marketing decisions. The publishing proposal will be described and illustrated. Illustrations and descriptions of a monthly and annual operating statement, a balance sheet. What smaller publishers need to know if they are to relate to a bank officer in getting and maintaining their line of credit. The fulfillment of orders, described with special emphasis on the customer service aspect of order processing.

PART V — MANAGEMENT

Chapter XV. The Role of the Manager

Primarily written for the manager, demonstrates the varying types of organizational structures to accomplish the mission of the publishing house. Defining the mission, planning, personnel matters, including salary and benefits. A "soft" section on techniques (how to motivate, evaluate, fire people).

Appendix

This will be a current list of reference materials. The text will have end-notes, referring to books, articles, and other materials that would slow up the narrative if included in the body of the book.

Sample Chapter

Fiction

After the editor has been captivated by your cover letter, read the summary, and (for nonfiction) the table of contents, she now wishes to see if you *really* can write the book. She turns, excitedly, to the sample chapter. This must close the sale.

The first chapter in a work of fiction must entice the editor to read on. The next chapter will show her that you can build and sustain reader interest. Editors prefer to read one or two chapters in sequence. In rare instances, it might be better to use a pivotal chapter which you feel is especially strong. After reading your chapters, she may ask to see the rest of your book, have it receive further consideration, and then, hopefully, recommend that the editorial committee buy the book. But to move in this direction, after reading only a sample chapter, the question that must be answered with a "yes" is, "Would the reader now wish to read the rest of this book and spend several hours with the author?"

To enable you to compare your work with the best, I have enclosed Chapter 1 from *True Grit*, by Charles Portis, as an example of a chapter of a fictional work that establishes tone and language, introduces vivid characters, and makes the reader interested in continuing. Read the first sentence and notice all the information it contains to get the reader off to a fast start. As you probably know, *True Grit* was a major best-seller in hardcover and paperback and later became an excellent film.

The first chapter introduces the narrator and heroine, a fourteen-year-old girl, and sets up the premise of the book, the style, and the pace. The prose is simple, clean, and engaging. An editor reading this would know that she was about to publish a very special book.

True Grit

By Charles Portis

Chapter One

People do not give it credence that a fourteen-year-old girl could leave home and go off in the wintertime to avenge her father's blood but it did not seem to strange then, although I will say it did not happen every day. I was just fourteen years of age when a coward going by the name of Tom Chaney shot my father down in Fort Smith, Arkansas, and robbed him of his life and his horse and $150 in cash money plus two California gold pieces that he carried in his trouser band.

Here is what happened. We had clear title to 480 acres of good bottom land on the south bank of the Arkansas River not far from Dardanelle in Yell County, Arkansas. Tom Chaney was a tenant but working for hire and not on shares. He turned up one day hungry and riding a gray horse that had a filthy blanket on his back and a rope halter instead of a bridle. Papa took pity on the fellow and gave him a job and a place to live. It was a cotton house made over into a little cabin. It had a good roof.

Tom Chaney said he was from Louisiana. He was a short man with cruel features. I will tell more about his face later. He carried a Henry rifle. He was a bachelor about twenty-five years of age.

In November when the last of the cotton was sold Papa took it in his head to go to Fort Smith and buy some ponies. He had heard that a stock trader there named Colonel Stonehill had bought a large parcel of cow ponies from Texas drovers on their way to Kansas and was now stuck with them. He was getting shed of them at bargain rates as he did not want to feed them over the winter. People in Arkansas did not think much of Texas mustang ponies. They were little and mean. They had never had anything but grass to eat and did not weigh over eight hundred pounds.

Papa had an idea they would make good deer-hunting ponies, being hardy and small and able to keep up with the dogs through the brush. He thought he would buy a small string of them and if things worked out he would breed and sell them for that purpose. His head was full of schemes. Anyway, it would be a cheap enough investment to start with, and we had a patch of winter oats and plenty of hay to see the ponies through till spring when they could graze in our big north pasture and feed on greener and juicier clover than they ever saw in the "Lone Star State." As I recollect, shelled corn was something under fifteen cents a bushel then.

Papa intended for Tom Chaney to stay and look after things on the place while he was gone. But Chaney set up a fuss to go and after a time he got the best of Papa's good nature. If Papa had a failing it was his kindly disposition. People would use him. I did not get my mean streak from him. Frank Ross was the gentlest, most honorable man who ever lived. He had a common-school education. He was a Cumberland Presbyterian and a Mason and he fought with determination at the battle of Elkhorn Tavern but was not wounded in that "scrap" as Lucille Biggers Langford states in her Yell County Yesterdays. I think I am in a position to know the facts. He was hurt in the terrible fight at Chickamauga up in the state of Tennessee and came near to dying on the way home from want of proper care.

Before Papa left for Fort Smith he arranged for a colored man named Yarnell Poindexter to feed the stock and look in on Mama and us every day. Yarnell and his family lived just below us on some land he rented from the bank. He was born of free parents in Illinois but a man named Bloodworth kidnapped him in Missouri and brought him down to Arkansas just before the war. Yarnell was a good man, thrifty and industrious, and he later became a prosperous house painter in Memphis, Tennessee. We exchanged letters every Christmas until he passed away in the flu epidemic of 1918. To this day I have never met anybody else named Yarnell, white or black. I attended the funeral and visited in Memphis with my brother, Little Frank, and his family.

Instead of going to Fort Smith by steamboat or train, Papa decided he would go on horseback and walk the ponies back all tied together.

Not only would it be cheaper but it would be a pleasant outing for him and a good ride. Nobody loved to gad about on a prancing steed more than Papa. I have never been very fond of horses myself although I believe I was accounted a good enough rider in my youth. I never was afraid of animals. I remember once I rode a mean goat through a plum thicket on a dare.

From our place to Fort Smith was about seventy miles as a bird flies, taking you past beautiful Mount Nebo where we had a little summer house so Mama could get away from the mosquitos, and also Mount Magazine, the highest point in Arkansas, but it might as well have been seven hundred miles for all I knew of Fort Smith. The boats went up there and some people sold their cotton up there but that was all I knew about it. We sold our cotton down in Little Rock. I had been there two or three times.

Papa left us on his saddle horse, a big chestnut mare with a blazed face called Judy. He took some food and a change of clothes rolled up in some blankets and covered with a slicker. This was tied behind his saddle. He wore his belt gun which was a big long dragoon pistol, the cap-and-ball kind that was old-fashioned even at that time. He had carried it in the war. He was a handsome sight and in my memory's eye I can still see him mounted up there on Judy in his brown woolen coat and black Sunday hat and the both of them, man and beast, blowing little clouds of steam on that frosty morn. He might have been a gallant knight of old. Tom Chaney rode his gray horse that was better suited to pulling a middlebuster than carrying a rider. He had no hand gun but he carried his rifle slung across his back on a piece of cotton plow line. There is trash for you. He could have taken an old piece of harness and made a nice leather strap for it. That would have been too much trouble.

Papa had right around two hundred and fifty dollars in his purse as I had reason to know since I kept his books for him. Mama was never any good at sums and she could hardly spell cat. I do not boast of my own gifts in that direction. Figures and letters are not everything. Like Martha I have always been agitated and troubled by the cares of the day but my mother had a serene and loving heart. She was like Mary and had chosen "that good part." The two gold pieces that Papa carried concealed in his clothes were a marriage gift from my Grandfather Spurling in Monterey, California.

Little did Papa realize that morning that he was never to see us or hold us again, nor would he ever again harken to the meadowlarks of Yell County trilling a joyous anthem to spring.

The news came like a thunderclap. Here is what happened. Papa and

Tom Chaney arrived in Fort Smith and took a room at the Monarch boardinghouse. They called on Stonehill at his stock barn and looked over the ponies. It fell out that there was not a mare in the lot, or a stallion for that matter. The Texas cowboys rode nothing but geldings for some cowboy reasons of their own and you can imagine they are no good for breeding purposes. But Papa was not to be turned back. He was determined to own some of those little brutes and on the second day he bought four of them for one hundred dollars even, bringing Stonehill down from his asking price of one hundred and forty dollars. It was a good enough buy.

They made plans to leave the next morning. That night Tom Chaney went to a barroom and got into a game of cards with some "riffraff" like himself and lost his wages. He did not take the loss like a man but went back to the room at the boardinghouse and sullied up like a possum. He had a bottle of whiskey and he drank that. Papa was sitting in the parlor talking to some drummers. By and by Chaney came out of the bedroom with his rifle. He said he had been cheated and was going back to the barroom and get his money. Papa said if he had been cheated then they had best go talk to the law about it. Chaney would not listen. Papa followed him outside and told him to surrender the rifle as he was in no fit state to start a quarrel with a gun in his hand. My father was not armed at the time.

Tom Chaney raised his rifle and shot him in the forehead, killing him instantly. There was no more provocation than that and I tell it as it was told to me by the high sheriff of Sebastian County. Some people might say, well, what business was it of Frank Ross to meddle? My answer is this: he was trying to do that short devil a good turn. Chaney was a tenant and Papa felt responsibility. He was his brother's keeper. Does that answer your question.

Now the drummers did not rush out to grab Chaney or shoot him but instead scattered like poultry while Chaney took my father's purse from his warm body and ripped open the trouser band and took the gold pieces too. I cannot say how he knew about them. When he finished his thieving he raced to the end of the street and struck the night watchman at the stock barn a fierce blow to the mouth with his rifle stock, knocking him silly. He put a bridle on Papa's horse Judy and rode out bareback. Darkness swallowed him up. He might have taken the time to saddle the horse or hitched up three spans of mules to a Concord stagecoach and smoked a pipe as it seems no one in that city was after him. He had mistaken the drummers for men. "The wicked flee when none pursueth."

Sample Chapter

Nonfiction

A useful nonfiction sample comprises the first two chapters of *Where Angels Walk* by Joan Wester Anderson and published by Barton & Brett Publishers, Inc. This book was produced after editorial discussions between the author and her future publishers, who believed in its potential strongly enough to start their own company to publish it. As its best-seller status and subsequent sales demonstrated, it was indeed an excellent subject for a book. It helped usher in a boom in angel books over the next few years.

This model demonstrates the need for more than one chapter. Had Joan Wester Anderson initially submitted a cover letter, a summary, and a table of contents to an unknown publisher, the editor reviewing it might wonder how the author would handle the subject and sustain interest. Chapters One and Two, taken together, show her abilities amply. The opening anecdote demonstrates the author's ability to tell a story, her use of dialogue, imagery, language, and finally her ability to surprise the reader. The second chapter illustrates the thrust of the book.

■

Where Angels Walk

By Joan Wester Anderson

THE BEGINNING ...

A guardian angel o'er his life presiding,
Doubling his pleasures, and his cares dividing.

Samuel Rogers, *Human Life*

It was just past midnight on December 24, 1983. The Midwest was shivering through a record-breaking cold spell, complete with gale force winds and frozen water pipes. And although our suburban Chicago household was filled with the snug sounds of a family at rest, I couldn't be a part of them, not until our twenty-one-year-old son pulled into the driveway. At the moment, Tim and his two roommates were driving home for Christmas, their first trip back since they had moved East last May. "Don't worry, Mom," Tim had reassured me over the phone last night. "We're going to leave before dawn tomorrow and drive straight through. We'll be fine."

Kids. They do insane things. Under normal circumstances, I figured a Connecticut-to-Illinois trek ought to take about eighteen hours. But the weather had turned so dangerously cold that radio reports warned against venturing outdoors, even for a few moments. And we had heard nothing from the travelers. Distressed, I pictured them on a desolate road. What if they ran into car problems or lost their way? And if they had been delayed, why hadn't Tim phoned? Restlessly I paced and prayed in the familiar shorthand all mothers know: God, send someone to help them.

By now, as I later learned, the trio had stopped briefly in Fort Wayne, Indiana, to deposit Don at his family home. Common sense suggested that Tim and Jim stay the rest of the night and resume their trek in the morning. But when does common sense prevail with invincible young adults? There were only four driving hours left to reach home. And although it was the coldest night in Midwest history and the highways were snowy and deserted, the two had started out again.

They had been traveling for only a few miles on a rural access road to the Indiana tollway, when they noticed that the car's engine seemed sluggish, lurching erratically and dying to ten or fifteen miles per hour. Tim glanced uneasily at Jim. "Do not—" the radio announcer intoned, "—repeat—do not venture outside tonight, friends. There's a record windchill of eighty below zero, which means that exposed skin will freeze in less than a minute." The car surged suddenly, then coughed and slowed again.

"Tim," Jim spoke into the darkness, "we're not going to stall here, are we?"

"We can't," Tim answered grimly as he pumped the accelerator. "We'd die for sure."

But instead of picking up speed, the engine sputtered, chugging and slowing again. About a mile later, at the top of a small incline, the car crawled to a frozen stop.

Horrified, Tim and Jim looked at each other in the darkened interior. They could see across the fields in every direction, but, incredibly, theirs was the only vehicle in view. For the first time, they faced the fact that they were in enormous danger. There was no traffic, no refuge ahead, not even a farmhouse light blinking in the distance. It was as if they had landed on an alien, snow-covered planet.

And the appalling, unbelievable cold! Never in Tim's life had he experienced anything so intense. They couldn't run for help; he knew that now for sure. He and Jim were young and strong, but even if shelter was only a short distance away, they couldn't survive. The temperature would kill them in a matter of minutes.

"Someone will come along soon," Jim muttered, looking in every direction. "They're bound to."

"I don't think so," Tim said. "You heard the radio. Everyone in the world is inside tonight—except us."

"Then what are we going to do?"

"I don't know." Tim tried starting the engine again, but the ignition key clicked hopelessly in the silence. Bone-chilling cold had penetrated the car's interior, and his feet were already growing numb. Well, God, he prayed, echoing my own distant plea, You're the only one who can help us now.

It seemed impossible to stay awake much longer.... Then, as if they had already slipped into a dream, they saw headlights flashing at the car's left rear. But that was impossible. For they had seen no twin pinpricks of light in the distance, no hopeful approach. Where had the vehicle come from? Had they already died?

But no. For, miraculously, someone was knocking on the driver's side window. "Need to be pulled?" In disbelief they heard the muffled shout. But it was true. Their rescuer was driving a tow truck.

"Yes! Oh, yes, thanks!" Quickly, the two conferred as the driver, saying nothing more, drove around to the front of the car and attached chains. If there were no garages open at this hour, they would ask them to take them back to Don's house, where they could spend the rest of the night.

Swathed almost completely in a furry parka, hood and a scarf up to his eyes, the driver nodded at their request but said nothing more. He was calm, they noted as he climbed into his truck, seeming unconcerned about the life-threatening circumstances in which he had found them. Strange that he's not curious about us, Tim mused, and he isn't even explaining where he came from or how he managed to approach without our seeing him.... And had there been lettering on the side of the truck? Tim hadn't noticed any. He's going to give us a big bill, on a night like this. I'll have to borrow some money from Don or his dad.... But Tim was exhausted from the ordeal, and gradually, as he leaned against the seat, his thoughts slipped away.

They passed two locked service stations, stopped to alert Don from a pay phone, and were soon being towed back through the familiar Fort Wayne neighborhood. Hushed, Christmas lights long since extinguished and families asleep, Don's still seemed the most welcoming street they had ever been on. The driver maneuvered carefully around the cul-de-sac and pulled up in front of Don's house. Numb with cold, Tim and Jim raced to the side door where Don was waiting, then tumbled into the blessedly warm kitchen, safe at last.

Don slammed the door against the icy blast. "Hey, what happened?" he began, but Tim interrupted.

"The tow-truck driver, Don—I have to pay him. I need to borrow—"

"Wait a minute." Don frowned, looking past his friends through the window. "I don't see any tow truck out there."

Tim and Jim turned around. There, parked alone at the curb, was Tim's car. There had been no sound in the crystal-clear night of its release from the chains, no door slam, no chug of an engine pulling away. There had been no bill for Tim to pay, no receipt to sign, no farewell or "thank you" or "Merry Christmas...." Stunned, Tim raced back down the driveway to the curb, but there were no taillights disappearing in the distance, no engine noise echoing through the silent streets, nothing at all to mark the tow truck's presence.

Then Tim saw the tire tracks traced in the windblown snowdrifts. But there was only one set of marks ringing the cul-de-sac curve. And they belonged to Tim's car....

When Christmas carols fill the air and our worries regress in a temporary whirl of holiday nostalgia, everyone believes in angels. But it's harder to accept the likelihood that the "multitude of heavenly host" on that long-ago Bethlehem hillside has relevance in our lives too, that God's promise to send His angels to protect and rescue each of His children is a faithful pact, continuing for all eternity, throughout every season of the year.

Angels don't get much attention today. If the spirit world is acknowledged at all, it's usually the dark side, the bizarre satanic cults that are wreaking so much havoc, especially among our youth. Yet there is evidence that good spirits are also at work here on earth—combating evil, bringing news, warning us of danger, consoling us in our suffering...then vanishing, just as the angels did on that first Christmas night.

Angels don't submit to litmus tests, testify in court, or slide under a microscope for examination. Thus, their existence cannot be "proved" by the guidelines we humans usually use. To know one, perhaps, requires a willingness to suspend judgment, to open ourselves to possibilities we've only dreamed about. "The best and most beautiful things in the world cannot be seen or even touched," Helen Keller said. "They must be felt with the heart."

Was it an angel? Our family will never know for sure.

But on Christmas Eve in 1983, I heard the whisper of wings as a tow-truck driver answered a heavenly summons and brought our son safely home.

SEARCHING FOR ANSWERS

> We not only live among men, but there are
> airy hosts, blessed spectators, sympathetic
> lookers-on, that see and know and appreciate
> our thoughts and feelings and acts.
>
> Henry Ward Beecher, *Royal Truths*

Angels. What did I really know about these celestial beings? As a Catholic, I was certainly aware of their existence. During childhood, I had learned a prayer to my guardian angel, and in college I had studied the hierarchy of angels, the nine choirs, each with its own function and assignment. But after Tim's curious rescue, I began to research angels with deeper interest.

One of the first facts I uncovered was a Gallup poll suggesting that more than sixty percent of Americans believe wholeheartedly in angels. Although scholars differ about specifics, their existence is accepted by all three of the great Western religions—Judaism, Christianity, and Islam.

Angels are mentioned more than three hundred times in Sacred Scripture, acting alone or in great gatherings, carrying out God's commands, forming a heavenly court, and—significantly—protecting and bringing messages to people. They played crucial roles in the Old Testament, including the books of the Jewish Torah, and are cited frequently in the Islamic Koran. Socrates often asked his guardian angel for advice. Many famous saints, as well as Salvation Army founder General William Booth, claimed to have seen angels, and Abraham Lincoln said he felt their presence frequently. Celestial beings appear in the works of Dante, Milton, and Shakespeare, as well as in the works of contemporary authors.

As civilization evolved, so did humanity's understanding of angels. To early pagans, gods seemed either to be stars and planets or to dwell in the sky, so it was a simple transition to consider angels as winged spirits who could travel easily between heaven and earth.

Interpretations varied as time passed. Early Hebrews contended that the universe was a hierarchy, with God at the top and other entities radiating downward from Him. They believed that angels constitute the "court of heaven." In writings they referred to "the angels of God," and bene Elohim, "God's sons."

Christians believe that God made angels at or about the time He made the world (Saint Augustine thought the two acts of creation were simultaneous), but before He created human beings. They were given minds and wills, like us, but had no bodies. At some point, according to the Book of Revelations, some of the angels wished to be gods and there was a terrible battle in heaven. The defeated angels then became evil spirits, headed by Satan, who roam the world to this day. The Counsel of Nicaea in 325 declared belief in angels a dogma, but a later synod condemned the worship of angels.

Muslims also believe that angels were created before man. According to the Koran, when humans were fashioned as God's supreme handiwork, angels were required to bow down before them, an order that prompted Lucifer's rebellion. Before Muhammad united them under one religious banner of Islam, the Arabs had recognized many gods and goddesses and had seemed to include angels among them. Muhammad acknowledged Biblical writings, and thus included angels in his new religion. In fact, after being chosen as Prophet, Muhammad claimed to see a beautiful vision of Gabriel, who promised to guide him in his new role. Muslims believe that angels witness for or against people on the Day of Judgment, and that recording angels are present at prayer in the mosque and elsewhere.

My investigations revealed that, whatever their beginnings, angels have three basic purposes: to worship God, to serve as heralds between God and His people on earth, and to act as our caretakers, while never interfering with our free will. Saint Dionysius, Saint Paul, Pope Gregory, and others further divide angels into nine choirs, listed here in descending order, along with their main duties: Seraphim and Cherubim, who love and worship God; Thrones and Dominions, who regulate angelic duties; Virtues, who work miracles on earth; Powers, who protect us from demons; Principalities, Archangels, and Angels, who are ministers and guardians of people.

The four archangels best known to us are Raphael, Michael, Gabriel and Uriel. Their numbers seem to be infinite, though, and throughout history, others have also been named. One of the oldest shrines in Turkey is dedicated to Michael, who is considered a great healer of the sick in that nation. Although angels are extremely powerful, they are, of course, subject to God in all things.

Religions differ on specifics about angels: For example, most Catholics believe that everyone receives a guardian angel at birth, a life companion especially suited to one's unique personality. Catholic children learn a comforting little prayer to initiate "conversation" with their angel, and the feast day of guardian angels is celebrated on October second. Ancient Jewish angelology also taught the personal-angel theory. In fact, the Talmud speaks of every Jew being assigned eleven thousand guardian angels at birth! The various Protestant faiths hold divergent views, most believing that we shouldn't pray to angels, but that we may ask them to intervene for us.

As angels began to appear in art, around the fourth century, artists gave them wings in order to distinguish them from the apostles or other holy men and women. We also think of them as dimpled cherubs, or perhaps a white-garbed chorus, as on that first Christmas night. Survivors of near-death experiences, however, cite "bright beings of light" that they met along the way—a reminder that light, symbolized in artists' renditions by halos or luminous bodies, represents heaven and, perhaps, those occupying it.

In Scripture, many angels appear as powerful, fearless soldiers. But there are also Bible stories about men and women meeting angels in human form, angels who look just like ordinary mortals...actually, just like Tim's angel. The companion in the Book of Tobit and the strangers who visit Lot in Genesis are good examples. And did not Saint Paul admonish the Hebrews—and all who would come after them—to "show hospitality, for by that means some have entertained angels without knowing it"?

The more I read, the more I realized that far from being outdated, angels are part of today's world too. There are cities, sports teams, aviator groups, and charitable activities named after angels. Members of the national street safety patrol known as the Guardian Angels wear T-shirts with an emblem featuring an eye, wings, and a shield denoting, according to founder and director Curtis Sliwa, "angellike protection offered to everyone, even those who don't want us looking out for them." There is an Angel Collectors Club of America, a national association of angel lovers with its own newsletter and annual convention. Angel Threads, a children's boutique, operates in Tucson. There is an Angels in Heaven day nursery in Cleveland and an angel collectible mail-order business in Riverside, California. Toller Cranston lives in a Toronto house filled with angel paintings, mobiles, and other celestial art; this six-time Canadian figure-skating champion likes angels because, he says, "they can leave gravity behind."

Even Hollywood gets into the angel act on occasion. Who can forget Clarence in the movie "It's a Wonderful Life," a lovable, bumbling angel who shows a suicidal man (James Stewart) the value of his life and what would have happened if he had not been true to his principles? Stewart has always maintained that the role was his favorite. "Field of Dreams," while not specifically about angel spirits, made such an impact on movie-goers that the baseball field in Iowa where it was filmed still attracts thousands of tourists every year.

And consider the popular television series "Highway to Heaven," produced by the late Michael Landon. Landon played the role of an angel, Jonathan Smith, sent from heaven to persuade hurting people to help one another. The idea had come to Landon one day while, stuck in traffic on a Los Angeles freeway, he watched drivers angrily honk and yell at one another. If they used even a fraction of that energy on being kind, Landon mused, how the world could be changed! Soon he developed a series based on the idea that kindness, not anger, solves problems, with the central character an angel who could make mistakes but could also be a spiritual catalyst in people's lives.

But Hollywood is fiction. Were real angels still around today, still ministering to us by caress, whisper—or in human form? If this dramatic, unexpected, and marvelously loving rescue had happened to my son, would I find that others had similar stories? It seemed logical; since I believe God loves all His children with equal intensity, He would certainly tender to everyone the same protection he had provided to Tim. But maybe few of us recognized this help when it came. Or perhaps we passed such moments off as "lucky breaks" or "coincidence." I would have to dig deeper to find the answers.

But it was one thing to read privately about angels, quite another to ask someone, even a close friend, "Have you ever met an angel?" People vary in their willingness to trust the supernatural, I think. Many consider the idea of heavenly beings walking around helping humans as incomprehensible. We are, after all, creatures of the twentieth century's "theology" of scientific proof. Others agree that such an encounter might occur, that we live in a world where not everything is explainable in logical terms, but they maintain that real miracles wouldn't—couldn't—happen to them. After all, didn't one have to be exceptionally pious in order to qualify? And if I found people who had an encounter similar to Tim's, would they be willing to share it?

Taking a deep breath, I went to the post office and rented a box. Then I wrote to magazines where readers were familiar with my byline and asked that my letter be published: I am looking for people who believe they may have met an angel, I wrote. I am not talking about human beings who, because of kindly deeds, might rightfully be called "angels." I am talking about spirits who appeared in human form to give some kind of help. Please write to me at this box number....

A few of the magazine editors wrote back stating that they didn't publish letters of this kind. They either objected to having their pages used as a means of research or, I suspect, considered my request a bit too weird. From others, I received no acknowledgment. This could mean a decision to discard my letter—or publish it. But even if my request was honored, what if no one responded? What if readers laughed or, worse, said to one another, "That Joan Anderson used to be a nice, normal writer. But I think she's gone round the bend, don't you?"

I waited, kept looking for angel material, and, one day, saw one of my requests in print. A few weeks later I went to the post office, inserted my key into my rented box and gathered my courage. This was probably what people called "the moment of truth." Today I would discover whether Tim's event was an isolated occurrence—or whether we were members of a great and glorious community of people whose lives had been touched by a heavenly being.

I swung open the mailbox door—and stepped back in amazement. It was filled with envelopes.

The Bio

The author with extensive credits, especially of previously published articles or books, does not have a problem in establishing her credibility, especially when submitting an excellent book proposal. It is the author with limited background who must include as much as she can to illustrate her qualifications (though a bio should never be more than a page). Following are two samples of a bio—one in resumé form and one in narrative form.

The sample resumé bio provides the author's salient information, address, phone, and fax at home and at work. The college education, which in this case is in English Literature and Education, and her present teaching career are designed to give the editor confidence in the author's ability to write at an acceptable level. The fact that the author, Mary Carol Smith, has written published articles provides additional assurance that her writing could be commercially acceptable. Note especially that Mary Carol Smith includes her public appearance on television and radio as evidence that she would feel comfortable promoting her own book if required. The author who can effectively promote her own book on radio and television has a special skill that may tip the scales in her favor. When the editor looks at the entire proposal, likes what she has read, and reads this bio, she should be reassured and ready to consider the proposal favorably.

Some editors prefer to see a narrative bio much like the second sample as another measure of the author's ability to write effectively. Just make your bio the best you can and tailor it as much as you can to your book's subject. Bios are as different as the people they reflect. Remember, even if you do not have a long list of credentials, many who were self-taught, such as Abraham Lincoln, were also best-selling and long-lasting authors. He even became president of the United States.

Sample Resumé Bio

MARY CAROL SMITH

HOME:
1234 South 21st Street
Philadelphia, PA 19765

OFFICE:
Department of English
New Smyrna Junior College
Box 1234
New Smyrna, DE 65431

HOME TELEPHONE:
215-555-5674
FAX: 215-555-5675

OFFICE TELEPHONE:
307-555-6339
FAX: 307-555-9396

BIRTHDATE: July 4, 1952

EDUCATION:

North Carolina State University, Chapel Hill, NC
B.S. in Education, June 1974
M.A. in English Literature, June 1976
Additional Writing Courses, Tanglewood, Mass., Summer 1990,1992

CAREER HIGHLIGHTS:

Associate Professor, English
New Smyrna Junior College, 1986–present
Teach Freshman English and Creative Writing

PREVIOUS PUBLICATIONS:

Have written over 1,000 articles, some of which have been published nationally in *Ladies Home Journal, Family Circle, Modern Bride, Christian Science Monitor,* and *American Baby.* One article, "My Husband the Baby," appeared in *Reader's Digest.* While raising my two children, now almost adults, I wrote at home with reasonable success.

PUBLIC APPEARANCES:

While in college was a model, selected by Breck Shampoo for its national advertising.

As member of the Executive Committee of Planned Parenthood and in charge of the Outreach Program, I make speeches and appear on television and radio.

Sample Narrative Bio

ABOUT THE AUTHOR

Robert Sampson has been a fixture on the national golf scene for many years. In addition to playing for Cornell's national championship golf team in college, he played on the PGA tour for three years before leaving to cover pro golf for the *New York Times*. He is now a freelance writer and frequent contributor to *Sports Illustrated, Golf Digest, Esquire, Playboy*, and many other magazines, and for several years has been a TV color commentator for ABC's "Wide World of Sports." His first book, *The Great Game of Golf*, won the USGA award for best golf book of the year. He lives in Dallas, Texas, with his wife and two children.

The Book Proposal: Pulling It All Together

From what you have read you can assemble a proposal incorporating the segments described and illustrated on pages 48–50. Your proposal should contain:

- a cover letter
- a summary
- a table of contents (most important for nonfiction)
- a sample chapter
- a bio

In all, the author would send twelve to twenty-four pages to the publisher—certainly not a complete manuscript. The editors I interviewed agree—the shorter the presentation, the more likely it will be read.

The subject of this proposal is an exotic work of fiction concerning a man who believes he is Don Juan. The purpose of this sample is to demonstrate that a proposal even for a major work can be effectively presented in a modest number of typewritten, dou-ble-spaced pages (single-spaced here to save space), and to encour-age you to use this well-tested, successful method that is likely to attract an editor's attention and a positive response. The summary and the table of contents position the chapter.

October 26, 1994

Ms. Mary K. Wright
Doublemint Publishing
1234 Wrigley Blvd.
Chicago, IL 23456

Dear Mary K. Wright:

Byron, Shaw, Rostand, and Corneille wrote about him; Gluck, Mozart, and Strauss placed this legendary lover in music. And now, he appears in a modern contemporary novel, reinterpreted for today's audience. None other than Don Juan.

I found Byron's unfinished epic poem, *Don Juan,* so filled with love and joy that I have written a novel which will run about 100,000 words, *Don Juan De Marco and the Centerfold,* which puts Don Juan in the cen-ter of our culture.

Read how Johnny De Marco, aka Don Juan, goes from the cape, the Spanish hat with the tassel, the brocaded pants, the shiny boots, and the mask to dungarees and then back in costume to find his long-lost love, Donna Ana.

Please read the story synopsis, the table of contents, and a sample of my writing. Please feel free to call me at 212-555-6789 or use the enclosed self-addressed, stamped envelope to reply.

Sincerely,

Karl K. Klopfer

■

Summary

Don Juan de Marco *

The story opens with Don Juan de Marco entering his favorite restaurant. He is dressed in a cape, black silk pants, a brocaded vest, a Spanish hat with tassels on the brim, and wears shiny black boots. Of all the women there, he selects Victoria, a beautiful young lady, waiting for her male companion to join her for dinner. Don Juan sends her a bottle of champagne, whisks her away to his bedroom, makes passionate love to her, and returns her to the restaurant just before her escort arrives. We learn Don Juan is the greatest lover known, adored and blessed by the many women he allows to be with him.

The story shifts to downtown Los Angeles, where a man dressed as Don Juan sits beneath a billboard of a semi-nude woman in a bikini advertising a Mexican resort, high above the street. The man is about to jump to his death. The police circle the area and send for the psychiatrist on duty, Dr. Jack Mickler, who arrives and is lifted in a cherry picker to try to talk "Don Juan" down to the street.

Mickler is about to retire, an old hand at suicides, and pretends to be Don Octavio del Flores, an acquaintance of Don Juan, and establishes rapport. "Don Juan" explains he has conquered all the women in the world except the most beautiful, Donna Ana, who is pictured on the billboard, and knowing he can never have her, he must die. Mickler convinces "Don Juan" that he may yet have Donna Ana, who indeed may be longing for him. "Don Juan" is taken by this logic and agrees to come down to the street in the cherry picker with Dr. Mickler, who then accompanies him to the psychiatric hospital at which Mickler practices.

Mickler is a successful psychiatrist married to a younger wife, Marilyn, of about fifty, who is finding life at the menopause period disturbing and loveless. They live together comfortably but not passionately. Mickler is now only ten days from retirement after thirty-five years as the top clinician at the hospital. He finds "Don Juan" fascinating and asks for the opportunity to evaluate "Don Juan" as a patient. Under the law, the hospital has ten days to either commit a patient to an institution or release him.

*This model prospectus was based upon the book *Don Juan de Marco*, a novel written by Jean Blake White based upon a screenplay by Jeremy Leven. The summary was written by the author of this book. The Table of Contents, the Prologue, and the Chapter were written by Jean Blake White and are reprinted by her courtesy. *Don Juan de Marco* was released by New Line Cinemas as a major motion picture featuring Marlon Brando, Johnny Depp, and Faye Dunaway.

At first, Mickler's fellow therapists resist but when "Don Juan" himself says he will only speak to Don Octavio del Flores, the character Mickler assumed when he talked "Don Juan" down and prevented his jumping, the director of the hospital agrees to give Mickler the ten days to treat "Don Juan," whom they regard as a delusional patient.

In the first session, Mickler attempts to give "Don Juan" medication to combat what he believes are "Don Juan's" delusions. "Don Juan" challenges Mickler to listen to his story before he prescribes the medicine. "Give me ten days," says "Don Juan," "and if I do not convince you that I am really Don Juan, I will take the medicine." And with this, "Don Juan" sets up ten chess pieces, and says, "Each day we will move one piece to mark the time." Mickler agrees.

"Don Juan" begins to tell his story in the first session of therapy. As he tells the story, he says he noticed as a baby when he saw his mother, the beautiful Donna Inez, naked that there was something special about him. Then he found as he grew, girls danced attendance upon him. At ten years of age, he was brought into the church and the priests asked God to save the young Don Juan before it was too late. Apparently God did not hear the plea because Don Juan continued into his puberty to understand the beauty and sexual nature of women and that they desired him passionately, and he had a limitless appetite and ability to satisfy.

Dr. Mickler listens to what he believes are fantasies, and asks "Don Juan" about his real parents. Not pleased, "Don Juan" admits his father was Italian, Tony De Marco, the Dance King of Astoria, and his mother, Donna Inez, was Mexican, the only daughter of a wealthy landowner, who died along with Donna's mother when Donna was young. Donna took over the operation of the plantation and prospered. Tony De Marco, who worked for a pharmaceutical company, was transferred from Queens, New York to Mexico. Tony and Donna met, fell in love, and were married. Tony took over the plantation and became "el patron." Don Juan was born exactly nine months after Tony met Donna Inez. The first session of therapy is over and Mickler is confused, even more so when he finds that the entire female nursing staff looks with great affection on "Don Juan," as he returns to the ward.

In the next session, "Don Juan" describes his first love in poetic detail, ending with a statement to Mickler. "Don Juan" says, "There are only four questions of value in life. What is sacred? Of what is the spirit made? What is worth living for? And dying for?" And the answer, "Don Juan" says, "The answer to each is the same, Don Octavio. It is love." The talk of love is having its effect on Dr. Mickler, who at home meets sexual indifference. The grief in their marriage of many years has taken its toll despite the present aura that "Don Juan" has created.

The sessions continue and "Don Juan" tells the story of how he killed the man who killed his father in a duel and was so ashamed of his role that he forever wore a mask to hide his shame.

To check the reality of the story, Dr. Mickler visits "Don Juan's" grandmother with whom he lived. He is shown to Johnny De Marco's ("Don Juan's") room, which is covered with magazine photographs of mostly nude girls. Catherine, De Marco's grandmother, tells Mickler that her son, Tony De Marco, Johnny's father, is dead, killed in a car crash in Phoenix. He had never lived in Mexico, and she did not know the location of Johnny's mother.

Mickler confronts "Don Juan" in the next session. He says his grandmother is delusional, not he. When Mickler confronts him with a photo of the model Chelsea Stoker, whose picture he found on the wall in Johnny's room, "Don Juan" denies this and insists that the photograph is of Donna Ana, whom he loves deeply and has lost forever. Mickler tells him that it is not uncommon for men to fall in love with a photograph of a desirable model, seek to meet her, and failing this, to try to commit suicide. "Don Juan" accuses Dr. Mickler of seeking the easy solution to the therapy because his colleagues would think him delusional if he said he believed the story, accepted him as Don Juan, and discharged him as a rational person. "Don Juan" says he will prove that the picture is really Donna Ana.

At the next therapy session, "Don Juan" tells an exotic story of a trip, his time in a harem, and his being with 1,500 women. The story is told in vivid detail well beyond the bounds of a normal imagination, but he stops short of telling about Donna Ana, which he says is for a later session. What these exotic and sensuous sessions have done is to bring Dr. Mickler, Jack, to realize that he loves his wife and to seek her out for sex. He rediscovers his love and his ability to relate to her as a sex partner.

As the sessions continue, the ten days are almost up and the staff has decided, with Dr. Mickler's reluctant agreement, that "Don Juan" should be medicated to remove the delusions. At the beginning of a session, Donna Inez materializes in the room. "Don Juan's" mother testifies to the accuracy of all "Don Juan" has said. Donna Inez tells about the struggle in which Don Juan kills Don Alonzo to avenge his father's death, and therefore must wear the mask to hide his shame. Dr. Mickler challenges "Don Juan" by saying that it appears that in this retelling by Donna Inez, Don Alonzo was the lover of his mother. "Don Juan" is troubled, but the matter rests.

Finally, "Don Juan" tells the story of Donna Ana to Dr. Mickler. Don Juan is shipwrecked and cast upon the sea. Don Juan comes to an island. He finds himself on the beach. His is ministered to by this magnificent creature, Donna Ana. They fall in love. Don Juan finally is ready to plight his troth to this one person. She loves him, too. Before they can get married, Donna Ana says she must hear the story of the mask. Reluctantly Don Juan tells her the story. She then asks how many women Don Juan has made love to. She urges him to be truthful. He tells her the truth, over 1,500. Donna Ana is enraged. She tells him that she, too, has had many lovers, is not what she seems, lashes out at him and runs away ... forever. His one true love is gone. "Don Juan" asks Dr. Mickler if he believes that he is really Don Juan now that he has heard the story.

Dr. Mickler says he really does believe the story, and shows his agreement by saying he is really Don Octavio del Flores, wed to the great and gentle beauty, Donna Lucita. "Don Juan" takes off his mask and hugs the doctor. Since he is believed, "Don Juan" is then willing to take the medication to remove the delusions. Dr. Mickler says he will return in two days to say goodbye on his last day in the hospital.

Dr. Mickler goes home and convinces his wife, Marilyn, whom he tenderly calls Donna Lucita, that they must liquidate all they own. He returns to the hospital where the medicated "Don Juan" is now dressed in blue jeans and is walking around in a daze. "Don Juan" is then brought to a commitment hearing, required by law before he can be committed. "Don Juan" tells the judge that he is really Johnny De Marco, grew up in Phoenix, fell in love with the centerfold, tried to kill himself, but now realizes that this was an irrational thing to do. The judge says it sounds as though Johnny is cured of his delusion, and discharges him.

When Dr. Mickler returns for the farewell to Johnny, he finds him dressed in blue jeans, ready to go home. He puts Johnny into his car, takes out a bag with his cape and other clothing and gives it to Johnny. They drive to Dr. Mickler's home. At his house, movers are cleaning out all its contents. Jack, his wife, and Johnny drive away to the airport, where they board a plane which takes them to an island that is the island "Don Juan" described in his therapy. When they arrive at the island, Johnny dresses in his Don Juan clothes. Dr. Mickler and Marilyn bring him to the beach and Johnny runs off into the distance, as Marilyn turns to Dr. Mickler and says, "Are you absolutely sure about this, Jack?" They watch as "Don Juan" and Donna Ana embrace.

TABLE OF CONTENTS

Prologue   The Legend

CHAPTER 1   Don Juan at Home

CHAPTER 2   Victoria

CHAPTER 3   Dr. Jack

CHAPTER 4   Marilyn

CHAPTER 5   Asylum

CHAPTER 6   The Chessmen

CHAPTER 7   Doña Inez

CHAPTER 8   Nurses

CHAPTER 9   Doña Julia

CHAPTER 10   Marilyn

CHAPTER 11   Don Antonio

CHAPTER 12   Catherine

CHAPTER 13   Voyagers

CHAPTER 14   Bernard

CHAPTER 15   Bootsie

CHAPTER 16   Marilyn

CHAPTER 17   Paradise

CHAPTER 18   Retreat

CHAPTER 19   Doña Inez

CHAPTER 20   Donna Ana

CHAPTER 21   Earth

CHAPTER 22   Marilyn

CHAPTER 23   Judgment

CHAPTER 24   The Island

DON JUAN DE MARCO

Prologue: The Legend

The origin of the Don Juan legend is obscure, but its essentials have been cherished for centuries. Don Juan himself was supposed to be Spanish, Italian, or Portuguese. His legend, however, was elaborated by the English, a colder nation but one passionately desirous of warmth. After all, Queen Victoria's Empire eventually included a great many palm trees, idyllic islands, and warm-water harbors.

England also produced the works of the warm-blooded romantic and charmingly susceptible George Gordon, Lord Byron, who was given to romantic adventures of various kinds, beginning at a very early age. He loved Greek islands—and a large number of women. He was the author of *Don Juan*, a long and skillful retelling of the legend in verse, satirical but sweet. Some Englishmen, even today, have memorized large swatches of the poem and will whisper it to an appreciative young woman if the setting is just right and the mood sufficiently intoxicating.

The other man who kept the Don Juan legend alive was Wolfgang Amadeus Mozart, the composer of the opera *Don Giovanni,* in which the wicked but adorable Don Juan is consumed by the flames of Hell, defiant to the last. Few men can hum the great themes of this opera, but no one who has ever seen it can forget Don Juan's final repudiation of responsibility and repentance.

In both tellings of the legend, women in great numbers find the don utterly irresistible. His charm is overpowering, his attractions without equal. He never intends to harm anyone, and though he keeps track of his totals, is not so much interested in scores as in playing well. He never thinks of himself as aggressive but as agreeable.

Don Juan never grew old, having been consumed by infernal flames long before wrinkles and gray hair could set in. In the legend, he remains forever boyish. Neither Don Juan's composer nor his poet ever reached, or perhaps wished to reach, middle age. Mozart died at the age of thirty-five. Byron died in Greece at thirty-six. Both fortunately expired before the prudish realm of Queen Victoria ever got underway.

We all recognize the legend's devotee when we meet him at a party or in a conference room, or even in advertisements in the personals sections of newspapers, though these days he is seldom equipped with a mask or sword or cape; he may even be detected masquerading in a thoroughly unboyish but enthusiastic body. He is often charming but growing cagier every day as women become more prone to laughter. His yearnings are quaint and his intense attachment to the past is rather touching. We must treat him tenderly, knowing so well that he's an antique. Like baseball cards or the book of Kells, he is to be preserved and lovingly appreciated but never to be played with again. However, Don Juan and his heirs do not, necessarily, yield gracefully to life on the shelf.

And thereby hangs our tale.

Chapter 1: Don Juan at Home

In which Don Juan prepares for death.

Slender, young, and languid, Don Juan de Marco reclined alone in a bedroom clearly designed for seduction. His pajamas were silk, and his mask was new. He lay on red satin sheets, reflected in many mirrors. A small fire blazed in the marble fireplace, in front of which a magnificent wolfskin covered the hand-knotted Turkish carpet.

A leather notebook, a slim journal without a title, rested on Don Juan's knees. He was writing his suicide note. Sad songs played on his stereo, which would normally have been pouring out mariachi music, tangos, sambas, or seductive arias from Italian operas.

He had started writing his suicide note more than a month ago. Although his life was short, it had been eventful. He wished to do it justice in his swan song, and justice meant the inclusion of many luscious women and exotic lands, discoveries and losses, and tales of narrow escapes.

He had finally reached the point where it became necessary to explain his reasons for wishing to die. He took up his richly engraved gold pen and began to write.

> I wish to end my life because of a broken heart. The woman responsible for this wish is Donna Ana, my glorious but lost soulmate. A world in which I must live without my darling Donna Ana is one in which I no longer wish to linger, even though I am still the world's greatest lover. I have made love to over a thousand women, a remarkable record for a man of my admittedly tender years.

The thought of the thousand beautiful women made him pause briefly. A tender smile played over his handsome features. His mouth was soft, formed like a cupid's bow. His cheeks were smooth, but since he had achieved his majority, he wore a modest beard and a dashing mustache. His hair was long and curled charmingly over his shoulders. He tapped the pen against his curved lips, a smile of rueful nostalgia continuing to flicker as he considered how best to state his story.

He began to write in a well-formed, calligraphic hand. He made no corrections and the words seemed to flow from his pen without effort.

Like music, gymnastics, or figure skating, the game of love occasionally produces a prodigy, blooming early and fiercely. I am such a prodigy. Zeus himself might have surpassed me in variety of species sampled, but never in zeal. No woman has ever left my arms unsatisfied, but that is of no great consequence now that I have lost the only woman who has ever mattered to me.

He arose from the tumbled sheets and put on a quilted dressing gown with a velvet collar, feeling that his sentiments required more formal garb than pajamas. Then he resumed his writing, a solemn expression on his gentle face, as he contemplated the end of his delightful stay on earth.

Thus, at the prime of my life, and the age of twenty-one, I have determined to end my life this very night.

He paused to consider the best way to proceed. He realized that the name and beauty of his beloved might not be known to the stranger who would read his note. Yet some understanding of his staggering loss was necessary if the situation were to be properly appreciated by that stranger.

The incomparable Donna Ana was once all my own, then was lost to me forever. I was shipwrecked, washed up on the shore like a bit of seaweed, found by a beautiful girl and cast again into the deep. Blighted affections, that's my problem. But as you read my story, stranger, think of a blazing beach, coffee and ouzo, and the burnished shoulders of a silk-draped, cherry-tipped virgin warbling innocently beside the amniotic waters of the Aegean.

You will say, of course, that after all, I had her. We grappled naked as the cruise boats sailed past. A hoopoe perched on the columns of the ruined temple, watching our acrobatic couplings with avian amazement. You will be puzzled by my determination to die, considering the net of lust we crocheted around our laboring bodies, the giving and taking and tasting and rolling over and over, shameless, and both as beautiful as sunfish. I surely had her, you will think, this boy enjoyed the fondest liberties, the most intimate secrets of his darling, and he possessed her completely.

Don Juan stopped to mop his brow. The room had grown much warmer. He shed his dressing gown and began to write the end of his note.

You would be wrong, you who judge me foolish, because for once and forever, she possessed me. There on the magic island, in the cool sea air scented with honeysuckle and thyme, in the shade of the olives, on the picnic table, she took what once was my heart and she threw it away.

Lewdness is no substitute for love. My genius was that I never gave less than both to any woman. Round or thin, blond, brunette or blue-haired, I drew out the best in every one of them, until an accident of navigation cast me up on that infernal beach, on which I wooed and lost my darling Donna Ana.

His mind was flooded by poignant memories of geraniums beside a white-washed beach house. He remembered the wonderful mornings, the delicious breakfasts—sausages and strawberries with Donna Ana beside the bluest possible waters, lulled by the sunlight and the pounding surf. He remembered the honey-flavored nights, the delectable midnight rambles along the moonlit beach. Happy though those memories were, he determined to stick to his task and complete his last document.

Now my love belongs forever to that single adorable woman. I will never again give my whole heart to every sweet lollipop the way I once did. Donna Ana owns me and she has run away from me, for no good reason. She has destroyed out happiness and left me only questions. Why did she trample on our perfect bliss? Why were my pleadings of no avail? Why was my most sincere sacrifice to no avail? Why did she flee from our Paradise without a backward glance? Donna Ana has given me my excellently good reason to take the plunge to oblivion, the dive into eternity. Memory, like a veil, obscures my eyesight, worse than my black silk mask ever was. I can no longer see a way to go on in this cold, cruel world.

He reached for his white silk handkerchief. His own prose and pitiful predicament had moved him to tears. He thought, with difficulty, of the pain his beloved might well be suffering. The thought gave him the strength to go on.

I don't know what she is feeling. I think she may be sorry, plowed under by regret. I'd like to think she misses me and that she finds all picnics dry and tasteless after the delicacy of our shared repasts. It would be pretty to think so. But I may never know whether she suffers as I do. That simple maiden to whom I gave my unstinting love may never have appreciated what a rare love she abandoned when she cast me aside."

A tear fell from Don Juan's eye to the page, blurring his words, making a perfect heart-shaped blot on the elegant page. He paused to dry his overflowing eyes and regain his composure.

Donna Ana left me only the ashes of love, left me alone to undergo the bitter pangs of rejection. Others may know this fearsome pain, the awful humiliation of being cast aside by a woman. I never had been turned down before that day. My life had been nothing but happiness and love, and the worship of women. All of them always adored me, and I them, until Donna Ana ran from me on that dreadful afternoon. After she left, I wandered the island for days. I was like an orphaned puppy, calling and calling her name. Looking under bushes and into caves, asking after her at the port, in every taverna, asking the tourists as they poured from the cruise ships, inquiring of sailors and old women in the village square, asking them had they seen my Donna Ana. Searching and searching, never finding her.

Don Juan's face reflected the agony of those days in which he wandered over the island, finding out too late that his darling had fled over the sea. The final discovery was too painful for him to write. He was almost done with his note. He wished the unknown reader to feel something of the delicate love that he had enjoyed, the tangible delights of the perfect woman.

Whoever finds this note, I beg you to keep the vision of that delicious and vanished woman hovering in your memory as she hovers forever in mine. Her image haunts my every waking moment, even more tantalizing to you, who have never seen her, perhaps, than to me, since I enjoyed the bliss as well as the blight. Picture to yourself the dimpled knees of the perfect nude, frolicsome in the sunlight of a tropical island, remember the scent of flowers and seaweed, taste the salt of a warm sea breeze and then imagine that it all revolves around you, that you are at the very heart of this feast for every sense and for the sentiments, that your every movement only increases your delight, that you are never tired, never hungry, never sad, but always bathed in bliss. Did I remember to tell you that her white silk gown flowed over her round sweet behind or her dainty feet so that she looked like a mermaid as she ran away from me? Did I tell you that? Too late now. I am for oblivion.

Don Juan closed the journal and put it on the nightstand, in plain view. He wanted to be sure the proper authorities would find it. Some well-trained, obedient, foolish detective was certain to poke around looking for clues to the fatal act, and would find Don Juan's swan song, his epic of a great love lost for no reason, his final confession. Of course, the plain, ordinary man could never be the same again after reading Don Juan's life story.

The young man smiled, thinking of the pleasure the unknown detective had in store for him, and the secrets of love he would uncover just by reading this slender book. The young man stood up and stretched, his silk pajamas rippling over his sinuous limbs, his resolve firm. He was prepared to die.

"But first," he declared, "one final conquest."

KARL K. KLOPFER

HOME: Telephone: 617-555-7567

1234 S. Lennox Avenue
Waltham, MA 09876

EDUCATION:

1966–1971   St. John's University, Annapolis, MD
               B.S. Fine Arts

1972–1977   Yale University
               Ph.D. Clinical Psychology

1978–1984   William Alanson White Institute
               Graduated—Psychoanalysis

EXPERIENCE:

1984–present   Clinical Director—New York Hospital
               Treated patients with multiple personality disorders.

PUBLICATIONS:

               Numerous papers for journals on multiple personality
               disorders.
               Novel: *Creator*, published by Putnam, 1972
               Novel: *Satan*, published by Knopf, 1977

OUTSIDE ACTIVITIES:

               Speaker at professional associations.

Summary

After reading this chapter, you should feel that you have been invited into a special seminar and been able to share with successful authors their secrets of success. Some of what you have read will be very useful to you—and some not at all. If you are able to use one idea or concept to make your proposal more effective, your time will have been well spent.

At the heart of this chapter is the advice: never submit an entire manuscript. Editors only sample manuscripts. Why allow her to choose a portion of your book at random? Instead, develop a proposal that takes the editor where you want her to go, describes your book quickly and deftly, and hopefully leads to a positive response. Provide enough information to give the editor a representative sample of how effectively you write and the organization of your ideas. This system of providing "just enough" succeeds because deep down, editors enjoy the thrill of discovering a new author and a good book. The talented editor wishes to be part of the creative process and establish a bond with you as you work on the book together. Submit enough of the manuscript to encourage her to participate with you in making your manuscript publishable.

8 The Editor and the First-Time Author Negotiate

■ Think positively! Be prepared to receive a call from an editor who has read your nonfiction proposal, or the summary of your novel, and loves it. She will invite you in to talk about your book (if convenient) and will then make an offer to acquire the rights to your work.[*] This offer is usually verbal and covers the essential terms of her proposal: the advance payment, the royalty, and whether it will be a hardcover or paperback book (or both). This is followed by the publisher's standard contract.

Most editors prefer to deal with an agent rather than directly with the author because a reasonably competent agent knows the "rules of the road," and speaks the same language. The editor has dual roles—she is both a sympathetic editor and a businessperson representing the publisher—and she would like to keep those roles separate. Often, however, the author may negotiate on her own. For first-time authors the money involved is often modest, and some good agents will not accept a beginning author unless he

---

[*] Publishers do not "buy" books. They acquire the rights to publish in the territory agreed on with the author and to license subsidiary rights to third parties on their behalf and on behalf of the author. The rights licensed may be sales in territories outside the U.S. and Canada, translation into foreign languages, etc. For a more complete explanation, see Chapter 9.

believes the author will be productive in the future. Other agents who do accept new authors do not always spend sufficient time making the best deal possible. An author negotiating for herself should, if at all possible, have a lawyer represent her, specifically a lawyer who is familiar with publishing and knows the dealmaking side of the industry. In any case, the first-time author should assist her representative by understanding the business and contract terms (Chapters 8 and 9 will help in this area). A knowledgeable client who is familiar with the realities of the publishing marketplace is a blessing to an agent, a lawyer ... and the editor as well.

While most good agents know the publisher's contracts and are experienced negotiators, a lawyer who is familiar with publishing is very helpful. This contract is a transfer of valuable rights from the author to the publisher, usually for her entire life and for fifty years thereafter. Both the publisher and the author obligate themselves to perform for the benefit of each other. A lawyer is important to ensure that the transfer of intellectual property, your valuable asset, is completed in accordance with the Copyright Act.

While the first confirmation that your book will be published may come in a telephone call or a letter, the real negotiation which precedes the drafting of a formal contract usually takes place in the editor's office. The editor has been provided with, or has developed on her own, a financial analysis that sets out the expected sales and returns, a tentative retail price, a manufacturing cost based on an estimate of the book's length and cost of typesetting, cover art, illustrations, if any, and overhead expenses. The financial director, in developing a system estimating profit or loss on a book, may provide standard percentages for sales, fulfillment, and other overhead costs to simplify the editor's analysis.

The actual "profit and loss" may be more complicated, but in general, this is what the editor might have as a financial guide:

The First Novel
by A. A. Author

75,000 words — Pub. Date Fall '96 — no illustrations

Estimated Retail Price. $20

Average Discount* 45%

Average Net Price Received per Book. $11

Gross Unit Sales Life of Book $30,000

Less Returns 33⅓% $10,000

Net Unit Sales $20,000

Net Receipts. $220,000

Mfg. Cost—Variable and Fixed. $109,000

Overhead (35% of Net Receipts) $77,000

Total Mfg. & Overhead $186,000

Net before Royalty & Profit. $34,000

Profit Target (10% of Net Receipts). $22,000

Available for Advance and Royalty $12,000

There are a number of methods to arrive at what the publisher believes he can afford to offer as an advance payment and royalty, and this is just one. Based on this example, however, the publisher would offer a $12,000 advance payment, probably one-half on signing the contract, and one-half on delivery of a satisfactory manuscript. In

---

* This is the amount by which the retail price is reduced or "discounted" when sold to a retailer or wholesaler. The resulting number is the average the publisher's customers (the booksellers) pay to the publisher. Thus, in this model, an average bookseller pays $11.00 to the publisher for a book. The discount is computed from the *recommended retail price established by the publisher*, not a discounted retail price which the retailer might establish on his own.

this case, the publisher is proposing to make an advance payment based upon his estimate of net sales for the life of the edition.

Although a royalty scale starting at 10% of the retail price and escalating to 15% is fairly standard in trade publishing, the author might be offered a low 6% royalty based on *net* receipts, the money the publisher receives from sales after it discounts the book. If the 20,000 unit net sales are achieved as projected, the author would receive $13,200 (6% of $220,000) in royalties, slightly more than shown in the preceding chart. A 6% royalty on *net* receipts is low, even for a first-time author, but to increase it would mean the publisher must accept less profit, fail to recover his overhead, or have to rely on income from subsidiary rights sales. (According to statistics prepared by the American Association for Publishers, most trade publishers fail to make a profit on their own sales and depend on sales of subsidiary rights to make a profit. Books with mass market paperback sales potential are sought after by editors.) The author, however, also receives a share of the subsidiary rights. For example, if the hardcover book were sold for publication as a mass market paperback, the author would receive more money.

Most publishers base their royalty on the "cover price" or recommended retail price. Net sales of 20,000 copies at recommended retail price of $20 would result in retail sales of $400,000; 6% of $400,000 would provide a royalty of $24,000. Basing the royalty on a percentage of *net* receipts rather than on a percentage of the cover price is obviously less advantageous to the author.

Now comes the negotiation. You, the author, are not aware of the financial analysis in the hands of the editor, and when you hear the proposal, the royalty may sound low to you. The editor also knows that the royalty is low but must be guided by financial analysis.

Let's assume you had heard that the standard hardcover royalties were:

> 10% of *retail* (not net) price on the first 5,000 net copies sold,

12^1/$_2$% of *retail* (not net) price on the next 5,000 copies sold, and

15% thereafter.

The editor is in a tough spot dealing directly with the author. She wants to maintain her relationship with the author, sometimes feeling closer to the author than to the publishing house, but her duty is to try to make a deal that is fair to her employer. The first-time author, even knowing this is an offer well below the royalty rate paid to established authors, does not wish to "blow" the deal, and so she is tentative about pressing her newly learned but imperfect knowledge. Often a third party is needed to encourage the editor to build an economic foundation for a better deal.

An experienced publishing lawyer can be very valuable in bridging this gap. Unlike those of an agent, the services of attorneys are readily available; they charge by the hour and assist in the negotiation of the deal and execution of the contract. It is likely that the additional money a publishing lawyer will generate in increased royalties and other concessions will pay for all or part of his fee. The publishing lawyer should know the economic rules of the road for advances and royalties for the genre of your book (romance novels, children's books, fiction and nonfiction for adults). If the lawyer can improve the money aspects of the contract and the book is successful, he will provide a better economic foundation for future deals. When the author starts with a lower than normal royalty rate and advance it is difficult to improve the economics for subsequent books.

Since I am a lawyer, you may think that my advice to seek a publishing lawyer to represent you is self-serving. Not true. Some of the clients whom I have represented are CEOs of major corporations who have negotiated million- and even billion-dollar deals on their own in their respective industries but realized they needed a publishing lawyer to negotiate their book deal. There is a list of intellectual property law firms shown in *LMP* and you should seek out a knowledgeable attorney, whether from *LMP* or on your own, to represent you. If you cannot find a lawyer where you live, you can use an out-of-town lawyer and communicate with him through faxes and telephone calls.

If you cannot engage the services of a lawyer, you should understand the editors' constraints, and try gently to move the advance and royalty rate up. Negotiating alone is not recommended; nevertheless, here is some advice which will be helpful.

As a first move, try to convince the editor that the book is likely to sell additional copies, especially if sales figures of similar books are available. Then point out that most authors receive escalating royalty rates of 10%, 12½%, and 15%. Suggest those areas of income from subsidiary rights sales (book clubs, foreign rights, etc.) that might provide more money to the publisher. Your objective is to introduce into the equation sources for additional income, either from larger than estimated retail sales or subsidiary rights, and to point to the "normal" royalty rates.

Realize there is always give-and-take in negotiation. If the editor balks at changing the sales estimate which would increase the advance, seek a higher royalty rate because the existing rate based on net receipts rather than the publisher's recommended retail price is at the low end of the scale. The editor may prefer to increase the royalty rate rather than increase the advance payment, since royalty rates based upon the retail prices are "standard." Have your calculator handy and have her explain what income you might expect under various royalty rates; it will demonstrate how the lower royalty rate affects your income and help you negotiate the best deal possible.

If concerned about making the best deal possible *and* maintaining your relationship with the editor, ask her to level with you and show you how she can improve the deal and still get it approved by her management. Most editors will help the first-time author, especially if they hope to publish subsequent books. But remember the editor works for the "house."

These are the money issues to be negotiated. The most important remaining points to be negotiated are the territories into which the publisher can sell the book, and the division of subsidiary rights income. I have outlined guidelines for a poor, fair, and good deal* in the hardcover fiction and nonfiction market which you can use in studying the deal you are offered. Royalties and advances are substantially different and lower for children's books, original mass market and trade paperbacks, and some reference books. One technique to establish the fairness of the offer made to you is to ask the editor how this offer compares with the average or best offer she has made. She will usually tell you the truth, and explain why, if true, your offer is less than the other offers.

A Poor Deal

- Hardcover advance is under $5,000.
- Hardcover royalties under 10% on first 5,000, $12^{1}/_{2}$% next 5,000, and 15% thereafter based upon recommended retail price (an even worse deal is the offer of an outright payment with no royalty).
- Trade paperback royalties under 6% with no higher royalty breaks.
- Mass market royalties are under 6% with no higher royalty breaks (there's usually one at 150,000 copies).
- Royalties based on the net receipts of the publisher.
- World rights in all languages. (For original romance paperbacks, this is acceptable if the author's share of foreign rights is 50%-75%.)
- Publisher gets more than 25% of British and translation revenue and more than 15% of income on first serial rights.
- Publisher gets participation in movie and television revenue.
- Publisher gets more than 50% of subsidiary rights income (book club, paperback, etc.).

---

* These deals originally appeared in *How To Be Your Own Literary Agent* by Richard Curtis (1983). The author has recently modified the deals to bring them up to date (1994). If the terms used are confusing, come back to this after you have read Chapter 8 or look for definitions in "PubSpeak" (Appendix B).

- Publisher is granted audio and new technology rights without a clear compensation schedule.

A Fair Deal

- Hardcover advance is $5,000-$20,000.
- Hardcover royalties are 10% of retail cover price on first 5,000 copies, 12½% on next 5,000, and 15% thereafter.
- Trade paperback royalties are 7½%-8% of retail cover price.
- Mass market royalties are at least 6% of cover price on first 150,000 copies, 8% thereafter.
- English language rights in the U.S. and Canada, U.S. territories and possessions.
- British and translation rights subject to author's approval, with author receiving 75% of income received by publisher when the publisher licenses the rights.
- Publisher keeps only 10% of first serial rights.
- Publisher has no rights in movies or television deals.
- Publisher shares all subsidiary publishing rights income, including new technology rights, with author on a 50-50 basis.

A Good Deal

- Hardcover advance is over $20,000.
- Hardcover royalties are 10% of the retail cover price on the first 5,000 copies sold, 12½% on the next 5,000 copies, and 15% thereafter.
- Trade paperback royalties are more than 7½% of retail cover price, with royalty break points to 10%.
- Mass market royalties are more than 6% on first 150,000 copies.
- English language rights in the U.S. and Canada, U.S. territories and possessions.
- British and translation rights subject to author's approval,

with author receiving 75% of publisher's income; if publisher does not license rights in two years, rights revert to author.

- Author retains first serial rights.
- Publisher has no rights in movies or television deals.
- Publisher may license audio and new technology, with 50% of income for publisher provided publisher pays an additional advance to author before licensing the rights.
- Author and publisher share income on paperbacks, 50% each on first $150,000, 60% to author on all income over $150,000. Payment of money received from paperback publisher to be paid by hardcover publisher to author thirty days after receipt, provided advance has been recovered.
- Income from book clubs and other subsidiary rights sales shared equally and paid thirty days after receipt, provided the advance has been recovered.
- Royalty rates are stated for new technology rights.

None of these terms are set in stone, and these deals are only meant to serve as rough guidelines in your negotiation. Most trade publisher-author contracts have terms that fall within the ambit of the Fair Deal. Favored authors and those with good track records receive all or a significant portion of the terms in the Good Deal category.

Do not be afraid to argue for a better deal. Some authors are so happy to be published, they accept an offer that is much too low and affect their future deals adversely. Remember that the editor, having come this far, really wants to publish your book. Be gently persuasive and persistent, but don't expect to receive everything you ask for on your first book. Your goal should be to get a bit better than the Poor Deal on your first book, move up the ladder and get a Fair Deal or better on the next book, and then get Good Deals for future books. It could happen.

9 Creating Contract Literacy

■ Unfortunately, after the editor has paid the author the greatest possible compliment by offering to publish her book, sometimes the author's joy can turn to sadness or, at the least, confusion when the author reads the publisher's "standard" book contract—eight or more pages printed in small type resembling a landlord lease and full of legal-sounding, difficult-to-understand terms. (Most of the text is "boilerplate," a legal term for the terms that are fairly standard on one publisher's contract.) Both sides know the standard contract is not standard. It can be revised if the author is a savvy negotiator and knows her rights and has some negotiation leverage.

In its most poetic form, a contract is a "promise" for a "promise." The author promises to deliver a book, carefully described, at a given date, which is her own work, and the publisher agrees to print, publish, and distribute the book and pay the author money if the book is satisfactory.

The publisher uses a long-form contract to protect his economic position and to cover contingencies that might arise. In agreeing to publish, he commits substantial sums of money and time. On her side, the author has already invested a year or more of her time in the book and wishes to ensure that the publisher will do his job. At the end of the day, business terms should be included in a contract which will enable both parties to be protected if they understand the "rules of the road."

This chapter is designed to help you, the author, develop contract literacy—to familiarize you with copyright law, explain legal terms, define the issues you will meet in the standard contract, and show you how to seek changes for your benefit. Most publishers prefer to have the author represented by an agent or attorney, who will review the contact on behalf of the author. Since the publisher's contract was drafted by a lawyer and the editor has a lawyer available, the law offers protection in some instances to a party to a contract who is not represented by a lawyer. Where a publisher's contract is unfair and where the author is not represented by a lawyer, should a dispute arise, the courts will often see that justice is done to the author.

When your book has been selected by an editor and the business terms worked out, it's almost a sure thing you will agree on a contract. However, as I have said before, no contract should be signed without the advice of a lawyer or agent familiar with publishing contracts and the Copyright Act. A good lawyer who knows publishing will not "blow" the deal or antagonize the publisher. He will make a deal fair to both sides and consistent with the law. If you become contract literate, you will save yourself time and money if you can understand the issues and respond sensibly to your lawyer.

Some publishers often have different standard contracts for paperback and trade, juvenile books, reference books, and so on. The essential terms are identical, since copyright law applies to all publishing contracts, but certain business terms may vary.

While, as you will see, there are many subordinate issues to be addressed, the main issues to be negotiated are the rights to be conveyed and money.

Grant of Rights

Under the current Copyright Act, the author is the proprietor (owner) of all rights in the literary work and all derivative rights (the right to put the work in print as a book). This is not a single right but a bundle of rights, owned by the author, starting with literary rights, and including film and dramatic rights and a long list of potential uses of the literary work in other forms, which are called derivative rights.

The author may grant all or any one of the rights; however, an exclusive grant *must be in writing*. Each right can be sold separately, but in real life, most of the rights that relate to the exploitation of the literary rights are sold together in a single transaction. Any right not granted in writing is automatically retained by the author. The "writing" can be as informal as a paper napkin used at the luncheon table where the deal is completed as long as the basic terms of the deal are written and it is signed by the parties. However, the "writing" is much more likely to be a multi-page document prepared by the publisher and submitted to the author after the author has verbally accepted the offer made by the publisher in a letter or by telephone.

The author's rights to be granted can be organized under "Form," "Language," "Territory," and "Time."

Form

Generally, the author grants rights to "print, publish, and distribute a book." It is better that the book be identified by its working title and a short description of the content. Most trade book publishers publish only in hardcover and trade paperback form. (The trade paperback is about the same size as the hardcover but has paper covers.) It is industry practice to grant both hardcover and trade paperback rights since almost all publishers have trade paperback lines. As you will see when payment terms are discussed, each type of book carries its own measure of compensation to the author.

Most hardcover publishers do not publish mass market paperbacks on their own. (There are major trade publishers who own mass market paperback publishing houses and offer deals for both hardcover and mass market paperback book rights in a single contract.) As we discussed previously, publishers who do not own mass market paperback houses will seek to have the author grant them the right to license the book to a publisher whose sole business is the publication of mass market paperbacks. The mass market edition usually appears one year after publication of the hardcover book. The rationale developed by hardcover publishers, to support their position in seeking to obtain and license mass market paperback rights, is that the hardcover publisher when he publishes his edition of the book establishes reader acceptance, which can then be exploited by the mass market paperback publisher. Because of his work and investment in launching the book, the hardcover publisher contends he should share the income from the paperback publication with the author. This concept is generally accepted, and it is normal for the author to grant the hardcover publisher the right to license the paperback and share the income, normally on a 50-50 basis. Major authors often command a larger share of the paperback income.

Most authors grant the hardcover publisher the right to license book club rights, and the income received from book club sales is almost always shared equally.

The normal grant language that the author should expect to see in the contract should read:

> The author hereby grants and assigns to the publisher the sole and exclusive rights to publish a work entitled "The Merry Month of May," a romantic novel of approximately 100,000 words, in hardcover and trade paperback under terms and conditions set forth below. The author also grants to the publisher the right to license others to publish and distribute the work in the form and under the terms as set forth under Subsidiary Rights in paragraph ___.

This language grants the hardcover and trade paperback rights to the publisher and authorizes the publisher to license other rights as specified, which would include the mass market paperback and book club rights as well as some other rights which are described later. If language contained in the standard contract is reasonably close to this sample, the author should be willing to accept it.

Language

English-language rights may be granted to the U.S. publisher. Some authors will retain the English-language rights for the United Kingdom and then employ an agent to sell these rights directly to a British publisher. The major differences in a grant occur in the grant of translation rights. Publishing is an international business and foreign-language rights are important and valuable. The publisher will seek to obtain translation rights for as many countries as possible. If the publisher has the ability to sell rights abroad on his own or through an agent, these rights should be granted by the author with a provision that would enable her to recover these rights if, after two or three years, the rights are not sold and translation has not commenced. (Well-established authors often retain the foreign translation rights and use an agent who specializes in selling foreign rights to sell them, allowing the author to keep all the income less the agent's commission.)

Language in the contract similar to the sample below is appropriate for a first-time author:

> The author grants the right to the publisher to publish the work in English and to translate or arrange for translation of the work in the following languages: *(list)*
>
> In the event, after two years from the date of the initial publication of the work in English, a contract has not been executed with a foreign publisher for publication in a language set forth above, the right to publish in that language will automatically revert to the author. Any contract or translation must provide for publication of the translated work not later than eighteen months after signing of the translation contract. All such contracts require the author's prior approval, which will not be unreasonably withheld.

In these typical paragraphs, the author has provided the publisher with the opportunity to realize additional income from the sale of translation rights which, of course, he will share with the author. If the publisher cannot arrange for a translation, the rights revert to the author and she has a chance to find someone to exploit the uncommitted rights. The sample paragraph also protects the author by requiring timely publication of the translated edition and her prior approval.

Territory

Since the author has granted the rights for publication in English, and English is a principal language in many countries, the territory in which the English-language book can be sold must be delineated. The most restrictive territory allocation is:

> The author grants the publisher the right to print, publish, and distribute the English-language edition of the work in *the United States, its territories and possessions, and Canada.*

The author may substitute broader territorial grants for the underlined portions. (The only issue is the ability of the publisher to exploit the rights in the territories granted by the author.) Some publishers will seek a territorial designation as *"English-language editions of the work throughout the world."* The reason for the publisher seeking an expanded grant is that there are large English-language markets outside the United States and Canada—the United Kingdom, Australia, and Europe, where English is often a second language.

Once again, the question to be asked is, "Can the publisher exploit this territory either on his own or by licensing his rights to another publisher?" In most instances, and especially now that there is a common market in Europe, the United States publisher will sublicense his English-language rights to a U.K. publisher. It is difficult for the author, especially the first-time author, to substitute her judgment for the publisher's, even one with limited overseas contacts. If the author does grant world English-language rights, she should reserve the right of reversion if contracts to exploit these rights are not entered into in a reasonable period of time.

Workable compromise language, as follows, could be accepted by the author:

> The author grants the publisher English-language rights throughout the world. It is the publisher's intention to enter into a contract for English-language publication in the United Kingdom, Australia, and New Zealand for sales of English-language books in these territories. In the event a contract is not entered into within one year after publication in the United States, the rights for publication in any country in which a contract has not been executed will revert to the author. Contracts for exploitation of these rights are subject to the author's prior approval, which shall not be unreasonably withheld.

Time

Rarely is there a grant for less than the term of the copyright, which is currently the author's life and fifty years thereafter. The Authors Guild has campaigned to have authors limit their initial grant to a term of twenty years, which would allow the author to recover and resell her rights upon the expiration of the term. The current copyright law provides for the right of the author to recover her book within a five-year period beginning in the thirty-fifth year. Thus, even under a grant for the life of the copyright, the author can recover her rights in a shorter term. The time and energy it would take to negotiate a shorter term for the hardcover or trade paperback is not worth the benefit likely to be achieved.

The shorter term is important when a license has been entered into by the hardcover publisher with a publisher of mass market paperback books. A successful mass market paperback might sell a substantial number of copies each year over an extended period. If the hardcover publisher, on behalf of the author, has the right to terminate the agreement after a 7- or 10-year term while the book is still selling well, the paperback publisher, who is generally interested in retaining the book, will pay an additional advance payment and royalty to be able to retain the book on his list. If not, there may be other publishers who would be interested in acquiring the steady-selling mass market paperback rights and might outbid the original mass market publisher. The trade press reports the resale of rights and renewals on a regular basis. One world-class author whose paperbacks sell in the millions, was well-advised early in his career and limited the term of his paperback license to 17 years. Because his books were very successful, he was able to renegotiate, when the 17-year term was almost over, some of the contracts on his early books with large additional advances.

Since many of the contracts for mass market paperback books are negotiated by the hardcover publisher, on his own behalf and on behalf of the author, the author should retain the right of approval of this and other contracts to be certain that all the terms including the grant period for the mass market paperback is significantly shorter than the life of the copyright. While it is not usual practice, the author might try to insert a sentence under the subsidiary rights provision to this effect:

> In licensing rights for mass market paperback books, the life of the license granted by the publisher shall not exceed ten years. All such contracts shall be submitted by the publisher for prior approval to the author, whose approval shall not be unreasonably withheld.

Sometimes, since the publisher has a strong bargaining position vis-a-vis the first-time author, she might expect to see in rare instances a contract provision like this:

> The author hereby grants the publisher the sole and exclusive right to publish in **volume** form in all languages throughout the world for the full term of the copyright as may now or thereafter exist the work, "The Merry Month of May," a novel of approximately 100,000 words together with any revised editions thereof, together

with the following subsidiary rights: (*the contract provision then lists eighteen separate rights concluding with* "any right not in existence now which may come into being in the future.")

In the illustration shown above, the author would effectively convey all her rights for her lifetime and fifty years thereafter. The words *volume rights* as they appear in this paragraph are what the lawyers call a term of art which the courts have determined to mean all formats ... hardcover, softcover, in short, any way the book can be reproduced and distributed. A first-time author, or even experienced authors, should resist this grant of rights because it is serious over-reaching by the publisher.

Money

Income from Advances

The author will be paid by the publisher for the exploitation of the rights transferred, by receiving royalties, some part of which is pre-paid or "advanced." This is how the term *advance* crept into the language of publishing. (It was originally intended for the author to live on the advance while he wrote the book.) An advance is usu-ally paid to the author by the publisher in installments: a portion on signing of the contract, perhaps another portion on submission of a segment of the manuscript, and a final portion on receipt of a "satisfactory manuscript." Advances may be paid in two install-ments for modest advances or, where there are huge advances, in ten annual installments. It is common for a modest advance to be paid half on signing and half on delivery of a satisfactory manu-script. Payments for larger advances are often paid one-third on signing, one-third on delivery of a satisfactory manuscript, and one-third on publication.

The publisher conditions all advance payments upon the sub-mission of a *satisfactory manuscript*, a concept that is over a hundred years old and which has been redefined by many recent court deci-sions. If the publisher rejects the manuscript as unsatisfactory, the contract usually provides for the advance to be repaid by the author to the publisher and the manuscript returned to the author. Repayment can be made either out of the author's current funds or from the proceeds she receives from a subsequent sale of the manuscript. However, the contract must state clearly the source from which the funds are to be repaid if the manuscript is unsatisfactory. Most publishers will set a deadline for third-party publication if they allow a first-proceeds clause. If the author does not sell her publication within the time allowed, the publisher will require the author to repay the advance from her own funds.

If the author fails to deliver a manuscript in a timely manner, the contract will normally provide for the advance to be repaid by the author. More about this later.

Income from Royalties

The publisher also agrees to pay a royalty as compensation for the rights conveyed by the author. This royalty is normally a percentage of the suggested retail price, but can be based on net receipts. (Royalty rates are generally, but not always, computed using the publisher's suggested price as the base. The fact that the retail price of the book is discounted by a retailer has no effect on this compensation.) For example, a royalty of 10% of the suggested retail price of $20 set by the publisher requires that the publisher pay the author two dollars for each book sold at retail. Royalty rates can escalate as the unit sales increase. The theory that dictates the practice of escalating royalties is that the publisher's plant costs are largest for the initial publication and the author should share this expense by receiving a lower royalty until these costs are recovered.

On a hardcover trade book, the rates of royalty are generally:

On sales of the first 5,000 copies	10% of retail
On sales of the next 5,000 copies	12½% of retail
On all sales over 10,000 copies	15% of retail

Trade paperback royalties are lower—usually 7½% to 10%, sometimes even lower.

Mass market paperback royalties are generally from 6% to 8%, except for major authors who may be able to command multi-million-dollar advances and larger percentage royalty payments. Children's books usually remain at 10% of retail until the sales reach 20,000 or 25,000 copies.

Income from Subsidiary Rights

The publisher also agrees to pay a percentage of the money received from licensing the subsidiary rights of the book. These amounts vary by the license granted. This is a typical division of income:

Right Sold	% to Author
Sale of mass market paperback reprint	50%
Book clubs	50%
First Serial Rights (Sale to a magazine prior to publication; often retained by the author)	90%
Second Serial Rights (Sale to magazine after publication)	50%
Microfilm rights	50%
Selections and Abridgments	50%
Electronic Rights (if sold within two years of signing the contract)	50%
Foreign publication license Outside U.S.	75%
Other rights	
Audio	75%
Translation	75%

*Dramatic rights	75%
*Movie and Television	75%
*Merchandising	75%

The rights for performance and merchandising shown with asterisks need not be granted to the publisher. These rights may be a major source of income for the author and the publisher is usually not well-equipped to sell them. The best advice to an author, new or established, is to retain dramatic and merchandising rights. Publishers have excellent subsidiary rights departments that sell most rights very effectively, but selling a book for a film or play or selling the rights for games or T-shirts requires agents who specialize in these fields. However, if your publisher insists on sharing in these rights, he should receive no more than an agent, typically 10%–15% of the amount of money realized from the sale.

In some contracts, the newest important right, electronic rights for use in CD-ROM and other new, often yet-to-be-defined technologies is missing from the list of receipts to be shared. Some publishers have made substantial investments in creating a New Media department and deserve the support of the author by a grant of these rights to the publisher. The publisher should be given a limited time to exploit the new technology rights, and then, if they are not exploited by the publisher, the rights should be reverted to the author, for her exploitation.

Method of Payment

In consideration for the grant of the rights, the author receives an advance payment—a lump sum, which may be paid in one or more installments as a prepayment of royalties. During the course of the contract, the author earns royalties based on the retail sales of the book and income from the various subsidiary rights. As royalties and other income are earned, they are charged against the advance. If earnings do not exceed the amount of the advance, most contracts provide that the advance payment is not recoverable. The contract should make this clear by identifying it as an "unrecoverable advance."

Despite the fact that every publisher, large and small, uses computers, the publishers make accountings to authors only twice a year followed by a ninety-day delay in payment. For example, a typical trade publisher will close his royalty accounts on October 31 and send the author a check based on the October 31 balance on January 31. This long delay has withstood attack from The Authors Guild, and it is changed only for major authors if the contract provides that large sums such as advances from paperback houses must be paid thirty or sixty days after receipt. A royalty statement sent by the publisher to the author will look in simplest terms something like this:

Royalty Statement
for _____ as of _____

DOMESTIC NET SALES FOR THE PERIOD

	Unit Sales	Retail	% of Retail	Due Author
	5,000	$20.00	10	$10,000
	3,000	$20.00	12½	$7,500
Total Domestic Sales	8,000			$17,500

SUBSIDIARY RIGHTS

Income Payment from Book Club $10,000 Total (your share $5,000)	$5,000
Total Income for Period	**$22,500**
Less Advance Paid Previously	($20,000)
Due with This Accounting	$2,500

The publisher's terms of sale allow his customers to return books if those books do not sell. The normal contract will contain a sentence which allows the publisher to offset a "reasonable" reserve for returns against current sales. This means that the publisher has in his judgment reduced the actual sales he is reporting to you to protect himself against anticipated returns. To define "reasonable," the following sentence should be used:

> The publisher may, prior to payment of money to the author, deduct a reserve for anticipated returns of not more than 35% in the first two accounting periods and 20% thereafter.

Satisfactory Manuscript

Before the author can obtain any of the benefits under the contract, the manuscript must be *"completely satisfactory in form and content in the sole discretion of the publisher."* These are the magic words that are used in most publisher's contracts. The concept, now redefined, that the publisher had an unrestricted right to accept or reject a manuscript based upon his sole judgment, was first upheld by the courts in 1899 when in the case of Walker v. Edward Thompson the court said, "The work ... is certainly as much a matter of taste as a suit of new clothes." For over three-quarters of a century, the courts permitted the publisher to reject manuscripts in his "sole discretion" without any reason other than his own "taste, fancy, or sensibility."

It was not until 1982 that the courts held that the publisher could not reject a manuscript arbitrarily in "his sole discretion" but was held to a good faith standard. The case that changed the practice involved Senator Barry Goldwater, who wrote a book, *The Conscience of a Conservative*, with a coauthor. The authors repeatedly requested editorial assistance from Harcourt Brace, the publisher, and received none. When the completed manuscript was submitted, the editor at Harcourt relied on the traditional satisfactory manuscript language in the contract and rejected the book, saying in her view it was not satisfactory. The publisher believed, based on precedent, that they could reject the book and recover the $60,000 advance paid to Senator Goldwater. Not so.

The court held that the publisher in good faith had a duty to edit, to review the manuscript, point out areas to improve, and assist the author to make the book satisfactory. Harcourt had refused to edit, and the court allowed Senator Goldwater to keep the advance payment and to recover his manuscript. The court also noted in the decision that by the time the case was tried, this "unsatisfactory" manuscript had been edited by another publisher, accepted, published, and had become a best-seller. Courts will refuse to order a publisher to publish a book, but they now consistently, if the rejections are in bad faith, allow the authors to retain the advance payments they have received and also allow the author to sell the book to another publisher without any obligation to repay the advance.

Additional court decisions have set out a course of conduct that an author should follow to avoid any controversy over the satisfactory manuscript. The publisher should be provided with an outline of the book and such other material to be certain that the publisher and the author are agreed on the nature of the book. This outline should be referred to in the contract, for example:

> ... the work, "The Merry Month of May," a novel of approximately 100,000 words substantially consistent with the outline attached...

Thereafter, the author should seek and use the editorial resources of the publisher, knowing that it is the publisher's duty to assist the author in improving the manuscript if possible. There have been cases in which the courts have held that where the editor has reviewed and proposed changes to a portion of the manuscript, and the author completes the manuscript on reliance of his encouragement, the publisher may ultimately reject the book but the author can keep the advance, retain the rights to the manuscript, and sell it to another publisher without repayment of the advance.

Reacting to court decisions, publishers are now stating their willingness to help make the book better in the contract, but they retain the right to reject it if, after all the revisions, the book is still not satisfactory in their sole judgment. The progress made on behalf of authors is that they can keep their advance and sell the book to another publisher if the rejection is not in good faith. Most publishers will insist on the now outmoded phrase *"completely satisfactory in form and content,"* but it is of no practical importance. Authors should not object to this phrase when it appears in the contract.

Subsidiary Rights

Most hardcover book publishers need the income generated from the sale of subsidiary rights (sales to paperback publishers, book clubs, etc.) to earn a profit for their publishing business as a whole. The hardcover publishing business is now and always has been a marginal business until the publisher develops a backlist (a list of previously published books that continue to sell with minimal expenses). Income from subsidiary rights is also crucial to the publisher, and the publisher will ask the author to allow him to exploit these rights. We listed the subsidiary rights when we discussed Money on pages 122–123. The rights being granted are described in the following pages.

Mass Market Paperback Rights

The most profitable subsidiary right for the author and publisher is the license for mass market paperback rights. The hardcover publisher will, at an appropriate time after publication, invite bids for the paperback rights. The paperback houses that bid offer a guaranteed nonrefundable sum payable as an advance against royalties. The sums paid for paperback rights for books by major authors may be substantial, many times exceeding $1 million. When the royalties on sales exceed the $1 million advance, the author and publisher receive additional payments. Books by first-time authors have also generated large advances for paperback rights. It is not unusual for the unheralded book that is well suited to the paperback format to generate bids of $100,000 or more. The advance and royalty are normally shared equally by the publisher and the author. Keep in mind, however, that only about one in four hardcovers is later reprinted in mass market.

Book Club Rights

When there is a major book, one that a publisher believes will be a best-seller, book club rights are sometimes auctioned in the same manner as paperback rights. The hardcover publisher seeks a non-recoverable advance and royalty from the book club. Suitable but not spectacular books are often sold through direct negotiation between the hardcover publisher and the book club without an auction. Sums paid for major books are in the hundreds of thousands. Normally this income, too, is shared equally with the publisher.

Magazine Rights

Some books, especially timely books or celebrity books, lend themselves to serialization in magazines or newspapers either before publication (first serial rights) or after publication (second serial rights). Traditionally, the author receives a large share of the first serial rights (and often controls them), generally 85% to 90%. Normally, income from second serial rights is divided equally.

Audio and Video Rights

There are now tens of thousands of books recorded on audio and video cassettes and sold by audio publishers. These rights now represent a growing source of revenue. Most publishers will insist that they be allowed to license these rights. Income received for the average cassette is in the thousands of dollars and they are rarely very profitable, except for best-selling cassettes such as the Jane Fonda exercise video and audio cassettes, where the income was in the hundreds of thousands of dollars. The author receives the major share of the audio and video income, often 75%. Since some publishers are still not adept at selling these rights, the author is best served by allowing the publisher a reasonable chance, possibly two years, to sell the rights and then recovering them automatically if still unsold.

Foreign Rights

As described previously, the publisher often contracts with a publisher in the United Kingdom to sell an English-language book into this territory. Similarly, the publisher may license foreign translations of the work. As discussed previously, there should be a grant of these rights for a limited period of time with the right to recover them if no deals have been consummated that will result in publication within a reasonable period. The net income from licenses granted under this provision is usually 75% to 85% for the author, 25% to 15% for the publisher.

Rights Retained

Rarely, if ever, should an author grant movie, television, or dramatic rights. Publishers include these rights in their contracts, knowing a sophisticated author will strike them out. They are not offended if these rights are excluded. With any remaining rights, the first-time author is best advised to be generous, but reserve the right to recover rights after a 2- to 3-year period if they are not exploited.

Early Payment

Money received by the publisher from the sales of subsidiary rights is included in the semiannual royalty statement. The royalty statement can come as much as nine months after receipt of the money by the hardcover publisher. It is not fair for the publisher to retain the author's share of this money for extended periods. In some instances, the publisher will accept an addition to his standard contract as follows:

> Notwithstanding anything to the contrary herein, the publisher will pay the author any money received for subsidiary rights sixty days after receipt providing the advance paid to the author has been earned.

Hardcover-Softcover Deals

Many of the major paperback publishers also publish hardcover books. It is becoming common for these publishers to buy hardcover, trade, and mass market paperback rights. The publisher pays one single advance, sets the royalty rate for each edition, and normally commits to publish in all three formats in sequence, or if he does not, he allows the unexploited right to revert to the author. The publisher prefers this because it is less expensive to buy all rights together even if he pays a somewhat larger advance than he would pay for hardcover-only rights. The author often prefers this because the money paid for all three rights is greater and she receives 100% of the royalties. Under a hard-soft deal, 100% of the royalties on the paperback are received by the author. In a hardcover-only deal, the hardcover publisher sells rights to a third party for a paperback edition, and the publisher and the author share the income equally. Authors who believe that the paperback income is likely to be greater than hardcover income accept hardcover-softcover deals.

Approvals

The publisher and the author are inextricably tied together in a joint enterprise to make the book successful. While many publishers may be reluctant to involve the first-time author in the publishing process, the author should have the prior right of approval for any contract entered into for a subsidiary right, for the cover and interior design, for advertising and promotion pieces printed to promote the book. (Admittedly, it is difficult for a novice author to secure such approval; what might be agreed upon alternatively is "consultation," wherein the author is consulted on such points and at least can give her two cents' worth.) The author should also have the right to approve in advance the sale or transfer of her contract to a third party. Unilateral action by a publisher may seem to be expeditious. However, involving the author creates a positive atmosphere leading to a long-term relationship.

Commitments on Marketing and Advertising

Every book receives marketing at the publisher's expense. Marketing might include catalogs, posters, exposure at conventions, mailings, etc. The publisher might also spend money on advertising and promotion in the form of print, radio, or television ads as well as author tours.

Unless the author is a major writer, the publisher will rarely include a specific commitment as to the amount of advertising or marketing money to be spent promoting the book. However, sometimes the publisher will write a side letter to the author setting forth the advertising and marketing planned and the money expected to be spent. Unless it is a book which the publisher believes can be made into a best-seller, the amount of advertising dollars to be committed is small—normally $1 a book (or less) based upon the initial printing. Thus, if the initial printing is ten thousand copies the entire ad budget is $10,000. Publishers depend largely on "free advertising"—reviews and author exposure on television and radio.

Warranty and Indemnification

Since the publisher relies on the author to prepare an original work and keep the text free from libel or invasion of privacy, the publisher will ask the author to warrant that the work is her own, is libel-free, and that she has not invaded the privacy of any individual. The publisher asks the author to indemnify him in the event of a claim or suit for infringement of copyright, libel, or invasion of privacy. There is almost no way for the author to avoid this warranty and indemnification. However, the author who does not have unlimited resources can ask that the publisher's libel insurance policy be used to cover her liability in the event an action is brought. The author can also ask to have the amount for which she is responsible not exceed the amount of the advance payment she receives.

Timeliness

As a part of the contract, the author promises to deliver her manuscript on a certain date. The publisher must commit to publish, usually twelve to eighteen months after receipt of a "satisfactory manuscript." The stricter contracts will state that "time is of the essence." This is a warning that timeliness is a precise obligation and failure to deliver on time will be a breach of the contract. This provision applies to delivery dates when the book is related to a time-sensitive event. For example, a book which is to be used in connection with a scheduled art exhibition must be delivered on the date promised. Failure to adhere to this date may allow the injured party to terminate the contract and sue for damages. Absent these circumstances, dates of delivery for manuscript and dates of publication can be extended and the contract amended accordingly. Publishers are generally amenable to reasonable delays if they know about them far enough in advance. An investment has been made in your book, and a book delivery a few weeks late is rarely reason enough to cancel publication.

Exclusivity and Option

Publishers usually ask for a one- or two-year period during which the author will desist from writing a book that will be directly competitive to the work covered by the contract. If this is a burdensome provision, an effort should be made to omit it or limit the scope of the exclusivity. For example, for a professor who writes regularly on the same subject for professional reasons, the promise must be surrounded with exceptions that will allow her to be productive. (While the author may be bound, it should be noted that the courts have held that publishers may publish competitive books as long as they continue to use their best efforts to promote the author's book.)

The publisher may also ask for an option on the author's next book. The publisher feels that he should have the first opportunity to acquire the next book written by the author before it is offered to another publisher. In arguing for this option, the publisher points to the effort and expense he will undertake in the book to be published. Authors should avoid making such a commitment, especially without having experienced the publisher's efforts on behalf of the book currently under contract. However, the clause can often be reduced to a first look at the manuscript, or detailed outline and sample chapter. Unless the parties agree to the terms, the author retains the right to take the book to another publisher—with no strings attached such as an option to match the highest bidder.

In Print and Termination

The author has a right to require the publisher to keep the book in print in a sufficient quantity to satisfy reasonable demand from potential readers. The standard provision obligates the publisher to do this. If he does not, the author may terminate the contract, purchase the materials that will enable her to reprint on her own at a favorable price, or sell the right to another publisher.

Remedy

It is in the author's interest to have arbitration as a remedy in the event of a dispute that cannot be resolved by direct negotiation.

Publishers will insist on using the courts to resolve differences, knowing the author has limited resources and could not finance the legal expenses. Publishers usually resist, but it does not hurt for the author to try for an arbitration provision.

You are now contract literate. This does not make you a lawyer, but it will make you a better-informed client. You should have a grasp of the rationale underlying a publishing contract, the terms used, the rules of the road, and what the normal commercial practices are, especially in terms of money you might expect from a publisher.

Your education continues when we review an actual contract and discuss it in the pages of Chapter 10. It is important that before you are asked to sign a contract, you have studied the terms of a typical contract. In some instances, material we have just discussed may be repeated and amplified to improve your contract literacy. Chapters 9 and 10, read together, should take the mystery out of the contract you will, it is hoped, be asked to sign.

10 The Contract Reality Check

■ Having completed your short course in contract literacy and negotiated the business terms of your contract, you are ready for the *real* contract—a daunting document.

Most publishers refuse to make their author-publisher contracts available for publication. Even The Authors Guild (which should be on the side of all unpublished authors) refuses permission to reprint their contract, one with excellent explanatory advice that would make any publisher's contract more equitable to the author. Access to that contract is a member benefit, and available only to those who join The Authors Guild.

With limited access to actual contracts, you should seek the counsel of a lawyer familiar with drafting and reviewing publish-|ing contracts. In addition, it is important that you see an entire publishing contract, study the terms on your own, and ask your attorney and editor to explain issues that may be troublesome or confusing. To introduce you to what you are likely to see, I have created a sample standard contract. While every publisher's contract will be different, the contract shown here is typical.

I have written this chapter as a conversation between you, the author (A), and your lawyer (L) to provide a feel for the process used to review and discuss a contract.

ABC PUBLISHING

AGREEMENT, made this ____ day of _____, 19___, by and between ABC Publishing, Inc., a New York corporation, having its offices at Pumpkin Ridge Road, Rye, New York 10580, hereinafter referred to as "ABC," and Mary K. Smith, hereinafter referred to as "Author."

WITNESSETH

WHEREAS, the Author has agreed to deliver to ABC a manuscript tentatively entitled, "HOW TO SUCCEED IN PUBLISHING" (the "Work"); and

WHEREAS, ABC agrees to publish or to arrange for publication of the Work and any revisions thereof, on the terms and conditions specified below.

NOW, THEREFORE, in consideration of the promises and covenants contained herein, the parties agree as follows:

A: This looks straightforward. Would you change this?

L: Yes, I would. As you recall, in order to provide a baseline to determine if the manuscript, as finally submitted, is what you and the publisher had in mind at the time the contract was signed, it is advisable to describe *How to Succeed in Publishing* by adding *"a nonfiction work of approximately 100,000 words consistent with the outline attached to the contract."* Should there be a dispute concerning whether or not the manuscript is satisfactory, this description provides the basis to determine the understanding of the parties at the time.

Because of the size of most conglomerates, many publishers have a series of imprints. Random House is an excellent example. In the same building bearing the name of Random House, you will find Villard, Knopf, and Pantheon, all trade houses with their own editors, support personnel, and areas of expertise. The imprint used may determine the care and attention your book will receive. Since this is the time to get these issues clarified, it is useful to identify the publishing imprint to be used when the book is published. If the manuscript is to be published by XYZ, a subsidiary or division of ABC, the party should be identified as "XYZ, a subsidiary of ABC" or "XYZ, a division of ABC."

1. Grant of Rights.

(a) The Author hereby grants and assigns to ABC, its licenses and assigns for the full term of copyright available in each country included within the territory covered by this Agreement under any copyright laws now or hereinafter in force:

(i) The exclusive right to print, published, distribute, and sell ("publish") in all languages in book form throughout the world and to license others to do so, a work now entitled HOW TO SUCCEED IN PUBLISHING;

(ii) The additional and subsidiary rights in the Work hereinafter set forth in 6 below;

(b) All rights to the Work not granted to ABC by this agreement shall remain the property of the Author.

A: This Grant of Rights clause is one I think I would discuss and try to get changed. It seems to me that I may not have any rights left. When I grant the right to "print, publish, and sell in all languages in book form" this means hardcover, trade paperback, and mass market paperback—everything.

L: You're absolutely right.

A: And when they add "in all languages" I'm granting English and all translation rights.

L: Correct again.

A: As I read this, I have granted them world rights on everything including subsidiary rights. If you add to this the phrase "for the full term of the copyright" it appears that this is an all-encompassing grant of rights forever.

L: All encompassing, yes; forever, no. You have the right to terminate the contract and recover the rights after thirty-five years. Nevertheless, this is a broad grant of rights.

A: What can I do to attempt to retain some rights?

L: Unless you are an important author, there is very little you can do. There are some openings in later paragraphs to ask for a reversion of rights if the publisher does not use them after a reasonable period. We will discuss these opportunities as we get to applicable paragraphs in the contract.

2.   The Manuscript

(a)   At the Author's own expense, she agrees to deliver to ABC on or before August 1, 1995, one copy of the manuscript and computer disks compatible with the publisher's computerized system suitable for a book of 100,000 words in length, satisfactory in form and content to ABC. The Author further agrees to furnish photographs, drawings, charts, illustrations, index, appendix, bibliography, and any other related materials (the "Related Materials") along with any written authorization by all third-party proprietors of copyrighted text and illustrative material contained in the Work and the proper forms of copyright notice for such material. (If the Author fails to obtain such permissions or provide such notices, ABC may do so and charge the cost to the Author.) All Related Materials will be in form and content satisfactory to ABC. If the Author fails to deliver any of the Related Materials or if the Related Materials are not in form and content satisfactory to ABC, ABC may obtain, create, or revise such missing or unsatisfactory materials and charge the reasonable cost thereof to the author. If retyping or reformatting the manuscript is necessary to make it ready for press, ABC may have it retyped and charge the cost of such retyping to the Author.

(b)   If the Author does not deliver a completed manuscript to ABC by the agreed-upon date, or ABC, in its sole discretion, deems the manuscript to be unsatisfactory in either form or content, then ABC may, at any time thereafter, serve a written notice upon him/her requiring him/her to deliver a complete and satisfactory manuscript. If the Author does not deliver a completed manuscript within thirty (30) days of the giving of notice or does not deliver a revised satisfactory manuscript within ninety (90) days of the giving of notice, ABC may terminate this Agreement at any time by written notice to the Author specifying the date of termination. If a termination notice is served, all amounts advanced by ABC to the Author pursuant to this Agreement shall be repaid to ABC by him/her and the Agreement will terminate as of the date specified in the notice. However, ABC may cancel its notice of termination any time before its effective date by simultaneously giving notice of its decision to cancel and returning to the Author any portion of the advance repaid by the Author pursuant to the preceding sentence.

A: What should I watch out for here?

L: This is a crucial paragraph. Let's discuss each element. First, the delivery date. You are committing to deliver the manuscript by August 1, 1995. The date can be changed by mutual agreement and most publishers will grant a delay. If you contemplate missing the deadline, be sure to get a written amendment to the contract. While the courts have ruled that whenever authors miss the deadline by a "reasonable" length of time, the publisher cannot terminate the contract, there is no need to leave yourself open to a cancellation of the contract, when most publishers will grant a reasonable delay.

You have agreed to furnish a disk and one hard copy. Be sure you will be able to provide the manuscript in a compatible software format. Ask the publisher to add specific words, such as "WordPerfect 5.1" or "Microsoft Word for Windows," etc., if that is what he has in mind.

You have also obligated yourself to provide, at your expense, all the illustrative materials, copyright notices, and permissions. If your book is heavily illustrated, you may be incurring considerable expense. Sometimes the publisher will share these expenses. Make sure you know the amount of potential expense, consider this carefully, and negotiate for cost sharing now.

Note that if you do not meet these obligations to the publisher's satisfaction, the publisher may obtain the materials and permission and/or re-format your manuscript to comply with his software, and charge this to you. The publisher may owe you additional payments, and these amounts could be deducted from money otherwise due to you. You should set a maximum amount that can be charged to the author.

Section (b) contains a very important concept. The phrase

to be studied is, "If ... ABC, in its sole discretion, deems the manuscript to be unsatisfactory in form and content ... ABC may terminate the agreements ... and all amounts advanced to the author shall be repaid to ABC." The courts have ruled that any such rejection of a manuscript must be in good faith and have, in their decisions, set standards to determine the publisher's good faith. This does not concern me because the words in the contract must be read with the implied condition of good faith.

However, I would try to have the publisher agree that if he rejects the manuscript, the moneys to be repaid can come from the "first proceeds" received on a subsequent sale of the book. This means that if the publisher rejects the book, the author may sell it to another publisher and repay the advance when he receives payment from the new publisher. Many publishers have specific language they use for this, and will amend the contract accordingly. Most publishers understand, realistically, that most first-time authors will have already spent the advance they received and do not have sufficient personal resources to repay the money before they sell the book to another publisher. Sometimes the publisher may only give you a year to find a new publisher, after which the publisher will require the author to repay the advance out of her own resources. If, however, you can get a "first proceeds" clause, and you probably can, it is worth the time it will take you to negotiate this change in the contract.

3. Proofs.

(a)   The Author shall read and correct his/her proofs and return them to ABC within [insert number] days of the proofs having been sent to the Author. Should the Author fail to return the corrected proofs within the allotted time period, ABC may publish the Work as printed with any changes or corrections as ABC deems necessary. All costs of the corrections and alterations in proofs (other than printer's errors) in excess of ten percent (10%) of the original cost of the composition shall be deducted by ABC from any sums due and owing to the Author.

A: This seems fair.

L: It is. You are on notice to correct proofs promptly and to be thorough. And this clause informs you it is too late and costly to make many corrections after the printer's proof.

4. Agreement to Publish.

(a) ABC agrees to publish the Work at its own expense with eighteen (18) months after acceptance of the final manuscript, except that this publication date will be extended to the extent reasonable and necessary in case of a delay caused by any circumstances beyond ABC's control, including, but not limited to, strikes, fires, shortages of labor or materials, mechanical difficulties, governmental restricts, and acts of God. ABC has the sole discretion to decide the Work's format, style of printing and binding, cover presentation, trademark, logo, imprint or other identification, retail price, and terms of sale, distribution, advertising, and promotion.

(b) If the Work is not published within the time period specified above, including any allowance for an extension due to circumstances beyond ABC's control, the Author may terminate this agreement by written notice which shall become effective six (6) months after receipt by ABC unless the Work is published before the expiration of the period. Upon such termination all rights granted hereunder will revert to the Author. Any payments already made to the Author under this Agreement in advances shall be his/hers to keep and the retaining of such advances shall be deemed to fully discharge all of ABC's obligations to the Author. No other damages, claims, actions, or proceedings, legal or equitable, founded on breach of contract, default, or failure to publish may be pursued against ABC by the Author or his/her agents, heirs, or assigns.

(c) In no event shall ABC be obligated to publish or have any liability to the Author for failure to publish (or any related cause of action) the Work when either the Author or ABC has been given notice of a claim, demand, or suit alleging that the Work (i) infringes the copyright or violates the right of privacy or any other right of third parties, (ii) contains libelous or obscene matter, or (iii) when the Author is unable or unwilling to verify statements in the Work purporting to be truthful or factual.

(d)   ABC will not be obligated to publish the Work if ABC's legal counsel is of the opinion that it contains unlawful material or material which may violate the rights of any person. If, in ABC's opinion, there appears to be a substantial risk of legal action or liability on account of the Work, the Author will make any necessary revisions or deletions to remove any such risk. If the Author does not make or authorize ABC to make the necessary revisions or deletions or if the Work is unpublishable in the opinion of ABC's legal counsel, then ABC may terminate this Agreement in writing any time prior to publication. In the event of such a termination, any and all amounts advanced to the Author by ABC pursuant to this agreement shall be promptly repaid by the Author.

A: Let me see if I understand this. The publisher agrees to publish eighteen months after he accepts the manuscript, unless there are circumstances beyond his control. Is this reasonable?

L: Yes, it is. However, I would not accept an obligation to publish in twenty-four months, which you may find in some contracts. Twenty-four months is really too long unless it is a long and very difficult book to print. Some art books may require an extended period.

A: Then, if he does not publish in time or, I guess, a reasonable time after that date, which is defined as six months, I am allowed to keep the advance payments and my manuscript, which I can sell to another publisher.

L: That is correct. If the publisher fails to publish, your only remedy is to be able to keep the advance payment and the rights to your book. You cannot sue the publisher for any income you might have lost by his failure to perform under the contract.

A: Let me say this once more. I have a manuscript which is satisfactory to the publisher. He fails to publish in eighteen months. I wait six more months and then notify him that I am terminating the contract. I have lost all this time when there may have been another publisher ready to publish my book, and I cannot sue for damages.

L: As they say in *My Fair Lady*, I think you've got it. However, in a real world, you monitor the publisher's progress. After you submit the manuscript, you should receive printer's proofs and some evidence of the book appearing in the publisher's next catalog. If there are no signs of activity, you should initiate a discussion which would allow you to terminate the contract according to the provision in the contract. This requires a new negotiation, but it is in the interests of both the publisher and the author to resolve this amicably.

A: I have no problem with the publisher refusing to publish if my book may violate the law.

L: Nor should you, as long as the determination by the publisher is based on a legal opinion.

5. Royalties and Advances.

(a) ABC shall pay to the Author royalties on sales, less returns, of copies of ABC's editions of the Work as follows:

(1) on all hardcover copies sold through ordinary channels of trade in the United States (except as otherwise provided below), the following percentages of the suggested retail price:

    (a) 1–5,000 copies: 10%

    (b) 5,000–10,000 copies: $12\frac{1}{2}$%

    (c) in excess of 10,000 copies: 15%

(2) on all hardcover copies sold in the United States at discounts higher than ABC's announced discounts for wholesale and retail accounts in the booktrade and (i) on a nonrefundable basis; or (ii) as special sales, as premiums, to catalog accounts, to book fairs, or outside the ordinary channels of the book trade, 10% of the amount received by ABC;

(3) on all hardcover copies sold outside the United States or for export to Canada or to other countries throughout the territory, 10% of the amounts received by ABC;

(4) on all paperback copies sold through ordinary channels of trade in the United States (except as otherwise provided below) $7\frac{1}{2}$% of the suggested retail price;

(5)   on all paperback copies sold in the United States at discounts higher than ABC's announced discounts for wholesale and retail accounts in the book trade and (i) on a non-refundable basis; or (ii) as special sales, as premiums, to catalog accounts, to book fairs, or outside of the ordinary channels of the book trade, 7½% of the amounts received by ABC;

(6)   on all paperback copies sold outside the United States or for export to Canada or to other countries throughout the Territory, 7½% of the amounts received by ABC;

(7)   on all large print copies sold through ordinary channels of trade in the United States (except as otherwise provided below), 10% of the suggested retail price;

(8)   on all large print copies sold in the United states at discounts higher than ABC's announced discounts for wholesale and retail accounts in the book trade and (i) on a nonrefundable basis; or (ii) as special sales, as premiums, to catalog accounts, to book fairs, or outside of the ordinary channels of the book trade, 10% of the amounts received by ABC;

(9)   on all large print copies sold outside the United States or for export to Canada or to other countries throughout the Territory, 10% of the amounts received by ABC;

(10)   on all copies of ABC's editions of the Work sold directly by ABC to consumers in response to mail order or other direct-response solicitations sponsored by ABC, 5% of the price paid by the consumer, exclusive of shipping and handling charges;

(11)   on all copies of ABC's edition of the World sold as remainders at more than the cost of manufacture, 10% of the amounts received by ABC; (ABC shall use its best efforts to give the Author notice of ABC's intention to remainder copies of the Work; ABC shall offer the Author 25 free copies of the Work, and give the Author a reasonable opportunity to purchase additional copies at ABC's manufacturing cost; however, ABC's failure to do so shall not be considered a breach of this Agreement nor give the Author any claim for damages);

(12)   on copies given to or sold to the Author, given away to promote sales or to charitable institutions, sold at or below the cost of manufacture or damaged or destroyed, no royalties shall be paid.

(b)   Only copies sold under 5(a)(1) shall be counted in determining the royalty escalations described in 5(a)(1).

(c)   As an advance against all royalties and all proceeds from the disposition of subsidiary rights due the Author under this Agreement, ABC shall pay to the Author the sum of $20,000.00 payable:

    (1) $10,000.00 upon execution of this Agreement;

    (2) $10,000.00 upon ABC's acceptance for publication of the complete and final manuscript for the Work.

A: I admit I'm confused. I do understand paragraphs (a)(1) and (a)(4) because the royalty rate is one on which we agreed, and paragraph (c)(1) and (c)(2) because this is the advance we agreed upon. But what about these other paragraphs, which seem to be reducing the rates of royalty for special situations? What is this all about?

L: It is confusing because there are so many exceptions. Basically publishers, by practice over the years, asked the author to give up some of her royalty payment if ABC must sell into a difficult market or if the publisher's income is reduced. The principle is sound, but the application of the principle places a disproportionate economic burden on the author's shoulders. Consider the case under (a)(2) when ABC sells "at higher than Publisher's announced discount" the author receives "10% of the amount received by ABC."

What this means is that if ABC sells a book with a retail price of $15 at the regular discount, the net received by ABC is $8.25 and the author's royalty at 15% is $2.25. If ABC, in order to make a large sale, increases his discount to 60%, on the same $15 retail book he would get $6 from his customer rather than $8.25 and the author gets $10 of the amount received or 60 cents as compared to $2.25 for a sale made at the full retail price. The publisher loses $2.25 in income; the author loses $1.65. By reducing the author's income, the publisher comes closer than the author to retaining its income.

Some publishers have changed this paragraph on their own, by reducing the royalty to the author in proportion to the loss of receipts by the publisher. Obviously, both the publisher and the author benefit when large sales are made, even at lower prices. And it is reasonable to seek to share the lost income, but to saddle the author with a disproportionate burden is believed by many, including The Authors Guild, to be unfair.

When you see this provision in a contract, you should do the arithmetic with the publisher and make an effort to get the percentage changed, but it should not be a deal breaker for you. Become a best-selling author and then the publisher might modify this provision in the next contract. The object of this negotiation is to get a contract, even though there are some clauses that may appear to be unfair.

6.   Grant of Subsidiary Rights.

(a)   The Author grants all rights as defined below to ABC throughout the world in all languages for the life of the copyright, whether such rights are exercised in whole or in part.

(b)   Definitions. The following phrases shall have the following meanings when used in this Agreement:

(i)   "Selection Rights" shall mean the right to use material from the work in the English language in abridged, adapted, and condensed versions in book form, on the radio, and in anthologies and other compilations in book form;

(ii)   "First Serial Rights" shall mean the right to use material from the Work in the English language in newspapers, magazines, and other periodicals including abridged, adapted, and condensed versions, whether in one or more parts (before publication in book form);

(iii)   "Second Serial Rights" shall mean the right to use material from the Work in the English language in newspapers, magazines, and other periodicals including abridged, adapted, and condensed versions, whether in one or more parts (after publication in book form);

(iv)   "Microfilm Rights" shall mean the right to use material from the Work on microfilm or microfiche and in information storage and retrieval systems or in connection with teaching machines, whether in machine or human languages;

(v)   "Print Rights" shall mean Selection Rights, First Serial Rights, Second Serial Rights, and Microfilm Rights;

(vi)   "Dramatic Rights" shall mean theatrical presentation rights, motion picture rights, television rights (including cassettes and other devices for home play), and any other similar mechanical or electronic visual reproduction rights including film strips, and any other method now know or hereinafter devised;

(vii) "Audio Rights" shall mean mechanical and electronic (other than radio) sound reproduction rights (including records, tape recordings, sound cassettes, and other methods now known or hereinafter devised;

(viii) "Merchandising Rights" shall mean the sale of rights for use in merchandise such as "T-shirts," etc.;

(ix) "Translation Rights" shall mean the translation from the English language to a foreign language;

(x) "Electronic Rights" shall mean recording or storage retrieval of text and illustrations by electronic or other means, the result of which serves as a substitute for the sale of a book;

(c) All rights in the Work not granted to ABC by this Agreement shall remain the Property of the Author.

A: If I sign this, it means I will grant all subsidiary rights for the life of the copyright to the publisher.

L: That is correct. There are a few major changes that should be made. First, I suggest you delete "Dramatic Rights" and "Merchandising Rights." It is customary for the author to retain these rights, because she probably will be able to get an agent who specializes in the sale of these rights to represent her once the book is published, especially if it is successful. Very few publishers have departments expert in selling these rights. As a consequence, they usually will relinquish them. Publishers of children's books who are familiar with licensing book characters often insist on retaining merchandising rights and should be allowed to do this for a limited period, probably two years. If the publisher has not exploited this right at the end of that time, it should revert to you. If, however, the publisher can demonstrate his ability to sell these rights, you may wish to give him the first opportunity to do this.

The publisher is normally well equipped to sell rights such as mass market paperback, book clubs, etc. However, I recommend that you negotiate a time frame during which they can sell these rights, say two to three years; if licenses have not been entered into by then, these rights would revert to you for your exploitation. This gives the publisher a fair opportunity, and then allows you to pursue this sale of the rights with an agent on your own.

7. Share of Receipts of Subsidiary Rights.

The amount received by ABC from the following rights shall be shared by the Author and ABC in the percentages indicated below.

		Author	ABC
(i)	Reprint Rights to Work in the English language in book form except by book clubs or like organizations	50%	50%
(ii)	Book Club Rights to the Work in the English Language in book form (whether full-length, abridged, condensed, or adapted versions)	50%	50%
(iii)	Selection Rights, except to book clubs or like organizations	50%	50%
(iv)	First Serial Rights	90%	10%
(v)	Second Serial Rights	50%	50%
(vi)	Microfilm Rights	50%	50%
(vii)	English Language Licenses in U.K.	80%	20%
(viii)	Translations in all languages	75%	25%
(ix)	Audio Recordings	75%	25%
(x)	Dramatic Rights*	75%	25%
(xi)	Movie and Television Rights*	75%	25%
(xii)	Merchandising Rights*	75%	25%
(xiii)	Electronic Rights	50%	50%

*Assuming these rights remain in the grant to the publisher; if not, strike through these items or any items excluded from the grant of rights.

A: All these splits look about right.

L: These subright splits are very standard and acceptable. The battle over the equitable division of electronic rights is still being waged, but if this publisher is making a major investment in developing electronic rights, he deserves the first chance to exploit these rights.

8. Royalty Statements and Payments.

(a) ABC shall prepare semiannual statements accounting for all payments due the Author under this Agreement. ABC shall send each such statement to the Author within ninety (90) days after the close of each period (January 31 and July 31 of each year) accompanied by payment to the Author of the amounts due to him/her for that period. If payment is not timely made, the Author may demand in writing that payment be made within forty-five (45) days. If ABC fails to comply, the Author may immediately terminate this Agreement and all rights shall revert to him/her.

(b) Each royalty statement shall report for each edition of the Work the number of copies sold (including total sales to date), the list price, the royalty rate, amount of royalties, the amount of reserve withheld for returns, and the gross amount received pursuant to each license, if applicable, granted by ABC. With each royalty statement, ABC shall send the Author copies of statements received by ABC from its licensees during the accounting period.

(c) Upon written request by the Author, he/she or his/her designated representative may examine, during normal business hours, the books and records of ABC insofar as they relate to the Work. If such examination discloses an error of five percent (5%) or more with respect to any royalty statement, ABC shall reimburse the Author for his/her costs of the examination; otherwise such costs shall be borne by the Author.

A: This looks straightforward. Is there anything that I should be concerned with in this paragraph?

L: You're right—it's a standard paragraph used by most publishers. The key issue here is the "reserve for returns" provision. It is a sad truth that booksellers and wholesalers return large quantities of books to publishers at their discretion, and it is appropriate for publishers to retain a sufficient amount of money to cover any possible overpayment of royalties to the author. How large a return is reasonable? You should try to have the publisher insert the phrase "up to 35% during the first year of sale and 20% thereafter." The rationale for this provision is that the returns are larger in the first year, and when a more consistent rate of sale is established the bookseller will order to meet his expected sales and have fewer returns. If you fail to convince the publisher to revise the language, relax; you can be assured that the worst result is that the royalties due to you in one period will arrive in the next period, a delay of six months.

A far more important issue is the payment of large sums that may be received between royalty statements. If you are fortunate enough to have your book achieve substantial subsidiary rights sales, significant sums ($100,000 or more) paid by a licensee could be held by your publisher for what might be up to nine months, depriving you of the use of your share of the money. You should be able to have the publisher insert a phrase that would require payments to you within thirty days after receipt of $100,000 or more, as long as the advance payment made to you has been earned. If it is unearned, the publisher can retain a sum sufficient to recover the unearned advance before he pays your share.

9. Copyright.

(a)   The copyright in the Work shall belong to the Author. ABC shall, within three (3) months of first publication, duly register a claim for a United States Copyright in the Work, in the name of the Author as "claimant." ABC shall print in every copy of the Work a copyright notice required by United States copyright law and the Universal Copyright Convention. Every license granted by ABC hereunder to reproduce and distribute copies of the Work shall contain a condition requiring the licensee to print the aforesaid copyright notice in all copies.

(b)   If the copyright in the Work is infringed by a third party, whichever party to this Agreement first learns of the infringement will inform the other. Author will have the right to join ABC in bringing suit against the alleged infringer. If the Author decides to do so, he/she will share equally in the expenses of the action and in any sums recovered as a result. Neither the Author nor ABC will be required to bring suit. Should one party decline to participate in a suit, the other party may proceed, bearing all expenses and retaining all sums recovered.

A: This looks routine.

L: There is the issue of the name in which the copyright is registered. Since the Author is the owner of the work, it should be registered in her name. You should make a note to check at the end of three months to be certain the copyright registration has been filed. Under the current U.S. copyright law, there is no requirement for registration, but there are significant benefits to the author and publisher from filing, should there be an infringement.

10.   Warranty and Indemnification.

(a)   The author hereby covenants and represents:

(I)   that he/she is the sole author of the Work (may use title of the Work in place of "Work") and is the sole owner of the rights herein granted and that he/she has not assigned, pledged, or encumbered such rights or entered into any agreement which would derogate or conflict with the rights granted to the publisher ("ABC") herein and will not do any of the above;

(ii)   that he/she has the full right, power, and authority to enter into this Agreement and to grant the rights herein granted;

(iii)   that except for materials of others, permission for use of which has or will be obtained by her/him, the Work is original, previously unpublished, and neither the work nor any material portion hereof is in the public domain;

(iv)   that the Work does not contain any material which violates any right of privacy, which is libelous, or which violates any personal or other right of any kind of any person or entity;

(v)   that the Work contains no material which would violate any contract of hers/his, express or implied, or which would disclose any information given to him/her on the understanding that it would not be published or disclosed;

(vi)   that no material in the Work plagiarizes or pirates any other work or infringes on any copyright, trademark, or other proprietary right; and

(vii)   that no recipe, formula, or instruction contained in the Work is injurious to the user or others [used only if applicable].

(b)   The Author shall indemnify and hold harmless ABC, its officers, directors, employees, and agents from any loss, liability (including settlements entered into in good faith), cost, damage, payment, or other expense (including reasonable attorneys' fees and disbursements) paid or incurred in connection with any claim, demand, recovery, suit, civil or criminal proceeding arising out of the breach or alleged breach of any of the foregoing warranties and representations.

(c)   Upon the receipt of any notice of any claim, demand, recovery, suit, civil or criminal proceedings which alleges facts inconsistent with the foregoing representations and warranties, ABC shall have the right to withhold any sums payable to the Author in reasonable amounts as security for the payment of his/her possible obligations pursuant to the indemnity contained in subparagraph (b) above. It is the intention of the parties that the right herein granted shall not be unreasonably or frivolously exercised by ABC.

A: What does this mean, really?

L: One of the main purposes of a contract, and one reason why the contract is so lengthy, is to anticipate future problems. Over the years, some authors have borrowed too freely from other copyrighted works, or they have based characters in a novel too closely on living persons and described these individuals in a way that might identify the individual and negatively affect the public's perception of the individual's character. The publisher has no way of knowing upon what sources the author has relied. As a result, he is putting you on notice in this provision that if you have infringed on a copyright or libeled an individual, you will be held financially responsible for these acts.

A: This could be thousands of dollars in damages and lawyers' fees.

L: True, but the remedy for this is to avoid copyright infringement and libel. Nevertheless, you should ask the publisher to cover you with his liability insurance if he has such a policy. Also, you should try to have your maximum liability, if you are sued, limited to your advance, another change in the contract many publishers accept.

11. Non-Competition.

The Author shall not permit or arrange for the publication, distribution, or sale in the Territory [defined in the Grant of Rights provision] other than by ABC, of any work which will compete with the Work or diminish the value of any subsidiary or additional rights granted by this Agreement except that the Author may grant licenses for the exploitation of any rights reserved to the Author under this Agreement.

A: I understand the need not to interfere with the publisher's ability to sell my current book by writing a competitive book, but suppose I still have to earn a living?

L: Your point is well taken. You should try to limit the time by adding "during the two years following publication." Add the phrase "directly competitive with the work and likely to diminish its sale" or seek to exclude books or articles required in pursuit of an academic requirement or writing in connection with your profession. You might mention to the publisher that he has the right, established by courts, to publish a book that might compete with *your* book as long as he continues to use his best efforts in selling your book. If he can compete, it might be reasonable to allow you to write another book as long as the book is not "*directly* competitive."

12. Option.

The author agrees to negotiate with ABC in good faith the same exclusive rights contained herein in his/her next written book-length work whether written under Author's real name or under any pseudonym ("Next Work") and shall submit an outline or the completed manuscript to ABC before offering such rights to any other publisher directly or indirectly. ABC shall have thirty (30) days after receipt of the submission within which to notify the Author of whether it will exercise its option with respect to the Next Work. If ABC notifies the Author of its desire to exercise such option within the permitted time period, the Author and ABC shall negotiate the terms of an agreement for a period of sixty (60) days commencing upon the end of the thirty (30) day period described in the preceding sentence. If a mutually satisfactory agreement is not reached at the end of sixty (60) days, the Author shall be free to offer said rights; provided, however, that the Author shall not enter into an agreement for the publication of his/her Next Work with any other publisher (i) upon the same terms or terms less favorable to the Author than those offered by ABC or (ii) upon terms more favorable to the Author than those offered by ABC without first giving ABC a further option to enter into an agreement as favorable. Such further option shall be exercised by giving notice to the Author within thirty (30) days of ABC's receipt of the Author's written notice of that offer.

A: This option clause concerns me. What if the publisher has not promoted my book or I cannot get along with the editor? Why should I be bound to this provision?

L: Most authors, and The Authors Guild, agree with you. To them it seems fair that you have the opportunity to seek a new publisher without giving your current publisher the opportunity to match a competitive offer, especially if the first experience with the publisher has not been satisfactory. It is very difficult to get a competitive publisher to give you an offer on your next book knowing that your original publisher can buy the book by simply meeting his offer. The publisher defends this provision by saying, "We like to keep our authors and we know each succeeding book is helped by the previous book." The compromise in language most acceptable to publishers and authors is to give the original publisher sixty days to make an offer, and eliminate the obligation to reveal any competitive offers, enabling you to accept what you believe is the best offer. If possible, the option provision should be omitted. A happy author will stay with a good publisher because it makes good sense to do so.

13. Out of Print.

(a) After receipt by ABC of a written notice, the Author may terminate this Agreement (provided, however, he/she is not in default or breach of the Agreement) if

(i) after five (5) years from the Work's initial publication date, all editions, whether hardcover or paperback, of the Work, go out of print; and

(ii) ABC fails to reprint or cause a licensee to reprint a U.S. edition within twelve (12) months after receipt of the Author's written demand. It is understood and agreed that ABC shall notify the Author within six (6) months of such demand of its intention to reprint or revert the Work. The notice to terminate shall become effective thirty (30) days after receipt thereof by ABC. All rights granted hereunder, except the right to dispose of existing stock, shall revert to the Author and ABC has no further obligation or liability to the Author except for his/her share of earnings to be paid when and as due. If ABC (or its licensee) shall have been prevented from reprinting by circumstances beyond its control including, but not limited to, strikes, fires, labor or material shortages, mechanical difficulties, governmental restrictions, and Acts of God, notice of termination shall be effective only after ABC shall have continued its failure to reprint for a three (3) month period after termination of the situation which prevented ABC's compliance with the Author's demand.

(b) The Work shall not be deemed "out of print" within the meaning of this paragraph as long as it is available for sale through normal retail and wholesale channels in either hardcover or paperback editions from ABC or its licensee.

A: Is there a problem in the Out of Print clause?

L: This is the clause usually used by publishers. The issue is whether the book should be considered "in print" if there are copies available in Persian by the Iranian publisher who has a license. The answer is obviously "no." This provision is made better balanced by defining that the book "is in print if it is available from ABC in hardcover or in paperback in the U.S.," or another definition that makes the book generally available in sufficient quantity to meet normal sales requirements in the main territory.

14.   Author's Property.

ABC shall be responsible for only the same care of any property of the Author in its hands as it takes of its own. The Author shall retain copies of the manuscript and any other documents or materials supplied to ABC. If the Author does not present ABC with a written request for their return, ABC, after publication of the Work, may dispose of the original manuscript and proofs.

A: This looks acceptable to me.

L: Yes, we're now getting into a series of paragraphs that are fairly standard and generally acceptable, so let's read through them quickly without comment.

15.   Author's Copies.

ABC agrees to give the Author twenty (20) free copies of the regular edition of the Work and five (5) free copies of any paperback edition published by ABC. The Author may purchase additional copies of the Work for the Author's personal use at a discount of forty percent (40%) of list price. The cost of the copies ordered by the Author will be charged to his/her royalty account unless there are not sufficient accrued royalties owed to the Author to pay for the ordered copies. In such case, the Author shall enclose payment with the order.

L: In passing, let me mention that some paperback houses will give the author thirty free copies of the book or a paperback original.

16. Licenses.

ABC agrees to promptly advise the Author of the terms of any grants or licenses made by it with respect to the Work whenever the Author's share of the proceeds or royalty is likely to exceed one thousand dollars ($1000.00).

17. Permissions.

ABC may permit others to reprint portions of the Work. Any payments received for such permissions shall be equally divided between the Author and ABC, however, ABC may grant permission without compensation to publish extracts from the Work containing 500 words or less in order to promote the sale of the Work. Such payment will be included as a separate item on the royalty statement.

18. Author's Agent.

The Author hereby authorizes his/her agent ("Agent") to collect and receive all sums of money payable to the Author under this Agreement. The payment to the Author's Agent shall fully and validly discharge ABC from its obligations to pay the Author such sums of money. The Agent may also act on the Author's behalf in all matters arising out of this Agreement, including, but not limited to, amendment of this Agreement and settlement of any controversies arising out of this Agreement. ABC may rely on the Agent in such matters until ABC has received written notice from the Author which terminates the agency. Upon the receipt of such notice, ABC shall pay all further sums payable pursuant to this Agreement directly to the Author or any other person(s) as the Author shall direct in writing.

A: How does this affect me since I do not have an agent?

L: You strike through (delete) this paragraph. But in case you do have an agent some time in the future, do not use this paragraph. All you need to do is have 10% or 15%—or whatever you agree upon as an agent's fee—paid directly to the agent and your money paid directly to you. You generally would not wish the agent to act on your behalf on all matters. You should be informed directly by the publisher of areas of concern arising out of the agreement and you will then consult your agent or lawyer as you see fit.

The following nine provisions are "lawyers' provisions" that should not concern you. They are necessary to make the contract complete and are useful if a dispute arises.

19.   Entire Agreement.

This Agreement contains the entire agreement of the parties in regard to the subject matter hereof, supersedes all prior agreements and understandings of the parties, and may be changed only by a written document signed by the party against whom enforcement of any waiver, change, modification, extension, or discharge is sought.

20.   Severability.

If any provision of this Agreement shall be prohibited by or invalid under applicable law, such provision shall be ineffective to the extent of such prohibition or invalidity without invalidating the remainder of such provision or the remaining provisions of this Agreement.

21.   Further Documents.

The Author agrees to execute and deliver to ABC any and all documents in proper or customary form necessary or helpful to the use, sale, license, or other disposition of any or all the rights granted to ABC herein, or for more fully carrying out the purposes and intent of this Agreement. The Author hereby irrevocably appoints ABC as his/her attorney-in-fact to execute any such documents.

22.   Notices.

Any notice required to be given, served, or delivered to any of the parties hereto shall be sufficient if it is in writing and sent certified or registered mail, with proper postage prepaid, addressed as follows:

To ABC:

ABC Publishing, Inc.
Pumpkin Ridge Road
Rye, New York 16580
Attn: Maureen Sheehan, President

To Author:

Mary K. Smith
605 Third Avenue
New York, New York 10158

or to other such address as a party from time to time may designate by notice to the other as hereinbefore provided.

23.   Remedies.

No course of dealing between or among the parties to this Agreement, any failure or delay on the part of any party in exercising any remedy of such party or any other party, or no single or partial exercise of any remedy hereunder shall operate as a waiver or preclude the exercise of any other remedy available to either of the parties.

24.   Survival of Rights.

(a)   In the event of the termination of this Agreement as elsewhere provided herein, any rights reverting to the Author shall be subject to all licenses and other grants of rights previously made by ABC to third parties as well as ABC's rights to the proceeds under those third party agreements subject, however, to payment to the Author for his/her share of such proceeds.

(b)   In addition to the rights set forth above in subparagraph (a), the following paragraphs shall survive termination: Author's Property, Warranty and Indemnification, Author's Agent, Assignment, Further Documents, Remedies, Notice, Entire Agreement, Applicable Law, Headings, and Royalty Statements and Payments.

25.   Assignment.

This Agreement shall be binding upon and inure to the benefit of the successors and assigns of ABC and the successors, heirs, and estate of the Author. Since this Agreement is for personal services, the Author may not assign or delegate any duties or obligations under this Agreement, however, he/she may assign any net sums due to him/her hereunder. ABC may assign this Agreement if it sells all or substantially all of its assets.

26.   Applicable Law.

This Agreement shall be governed by and construed in accordance with the internal substantive laws of the State of New York and the parties hereby consent to the jurisdiction of the courts over the matters relating to this Agreement.

27.   Headings.

The headings in this Agreement are for convenience of reference only and shall not limit or otherwise affect the meaning hereof.

Agreed this _____ day of _____, 199__, by:

_____
                                    Author

S.S.# _____

_____
                                    Publisher

L: Of all the "lawyer's provisions," the only one that I would try to change would be number 26, "Applicable Law." This provision means that any dispute that cannot be resolved by the parties must go to court, an expensive and time-consuming process. An easier course being followed by some publishers is to provide for arbitration, which can be done in an informal setting. The disputants agree on an arbitrator, they argue the merits of their case without a lawyer if they prefer, and the arbitrator makes a decision based upon fairness. If you could, I would suggest you try to get the following paragraph substituted for the paragraph shown above:

Arbitration.

Any controversy or claim arising out of or relating to this agreement, or the breach hereof, shall be settled by arbitration in New York City, in accordance with the rules of the American Arbitration Association. Judgment upon the award rendered may be entered in any court having jurisdiction thereof. The costs of the arbitration shall be borne equally by the parties thereto.

L: Finally, some advice about electronic rights. You may expect to see something much like this in the future:

Grant of Electronic Rights:

The Author grants to the Publisher the exclusive right to create, distribute, and license electronic rights as described below:

(i) the right to encompass or enhance any material or aspect of the work in a format as illustrated by a "floppy" disc, CD-ROM, or any other format now known or to be developed in the future.

(ii) the right to transmit the Work by broadcast, public display, transmission networks, or any other form of transmission now known or to be developed in the future.

(iii) the right to utilize any medium to reinterpret the Work in print, in an optical or graphical form, or in any other medium now known or to be developed in the future.

The Author agrees that should an electronic application of the Work not included in this grant become known, at the written request of the Publisher, the Author will grant the exclusive right to the Publisher and the compensation to the Author shall be determined by relating the new right to existing rights or, if this is not possible, by mutual agreement.

L: This is a provision currently appearing in some publishers' contracts. It has generated strong objection from The Authors Guild. The grant is sweeping and the payment terms difficult to administer. If the publisher has made a significant investment in a new technology effort, the author might profitably agree to this provision and trust that there will be a reasonable exploitation of her rights and a fair payment. If the publisher has not invested substantially in the new technology, the author would not be well advised to agree to this provision, but rather seek some modification that grants the author some degree of control over the dispensation of these rights.

At the time of this writing, the position of The Authors Guild in this matter includes three conditions: 1) fair compensation on the traditional advance and royalty basis, that is, payment per use or sale; 2) when rights are licensed by the publisher to another party, the author should be compensated by the publisher on the traditional basis of an agent's commission, with the author receiving 85% to 90%; and 3) no use of a work should be made without the writer's approval of medium, format, and content.

Electronic publishing is evolving rapidly and significantly, and the next decade should see more standardized terms in this area that are acceptable to both publisher and author. I advise the first-time author to ask for something similar to The Authors Guild's recommendation—and to be happy with what she can get.

A: What is your final word of advice?

L: Relax. The main issue is to get your book published with enthusiasm by the publisher. One good technique to eliminate many of the points of negotiation is to ask the publisher to make the changes he would normally make if the issue were raised by his best author. I have found that, in order to save the negotiating time, the publisher will often make some changes that will improve the contract to your benefit. The publisher wishes to maintain a cordial relationship with you because he hopes that there are many more books to come. Do not expect to get major concessions, but whatever you get, put these issues out of the negotiations. You can then concentrate on those issues that trouble you and ones not resolved.

Remember, this is only one book, and if you are successful you can always improve the contract in the negotiation for your next book.

A: This certainly has been an education for me. While I feel better prepared, I still think I need a lawyer.

L: I think you're right. However, with your increased contract literacy (from Chapter 9) and this review of a sample contract, you should be able to save the lawyer's time and reduce the lawyer's fee.

A: How many changes do you think I will be able to make in this contract?

L: As a first-time author, not many. The publisher realizes that he must continue to seek out and publish new authors. He also realizes that publishing new authors is a substantial risk. Publishers often lose money on first-time authors and, as a result, publishers wish to obtain the broadest grant of rights and the most favorable economic terms to minimize their risk. And if they have made a bad initial judgment in selecting the book and the manuscript, when received, is not satisfactory, they want to be relieved of their responsibility to publish the book at the least cost.

In general, most publishers are fair-minded and understand the role of the author in their future. If you can address the issues in a principled manner, explaining the merits of your position, you will find the publisher will meet you more than halfway. Go into the negotiations with a working knowledge of publishing law and a positive, open manner and you will get a fair contract.

11 Reprise

■ From the first chapter, the goal of this book has been to help you get your manuscript published. In this game, a silver medal does not count. Praise from an editor is not as meaningful as praise from a reader of your published book. Winners are those writers who are published.

This book has focused on submitting a quality manuscript and the Eight-Step Program for Selling Your Manuscript:

1. Write a Winning Proposal.

2. Find the Right Publisher.

3. Find the Right Editor.

4. Use the Two P's—Patience and Persistence.

5. Use Rejections Profitably.

6. Keep Moving. Make Contacts.

7. Think Small.

8. Keep Reading.

At this point, as our time together has almost come to an end, I add one more step:

9. Keep Writing.

If you continue to get rejections after having reworked your manuscript with help and researched carefully to find the right publisher and right editor, do not be discouraged. Keep your day job, but keep writing.

For solace, read *Rotten Rejections*, edited by André Bernard. If you are not succeeding at first, you are part of a fraternity of writers whose works were initially rejected. The list of those writers include: Stephen King, who was told the genre in which he was writing "would not sell"; John Le Carré, who was told he had "no future"; Norman Mailer, admonished that his writing would "set back publishing twenty-five years"; and Ayn Rand, who was advised that her work was "unsalable and unpublishable."

Rejection of manuscripts is a part of the publishing process. The tastes and sensitivity of editors vary. Public tastes change. Editors often have a difficult time explaining why they select a particular manuscript. They often say, "It just feels right."

If you feel strongly about your book, you can even do what Pat Conroy, the author of *The Prince of Tides*, did when no one would publish his first book, and self-publish.

Whatever you do, maintain a positive attitude and take the ninth step in the program to sell your book—keep writing.

The Tool Kit

These five Appendixes provide the tools you will need to be expert as an author-agent: They are:

A. PubSpeak—The Publishing Industry's Private Language; a Glossary

B. How to use LMP to Find Your Publisher and Editor

C. Best Bets—The Publishers Most Likely to Read and Accept Your Book

D. Manuscript Submission Record

E. References—Some Other Books You Might Wish to Read

PubSpeak–
The Publishing Industry's
Private Language

■ Publishers have their own special language, which I call PubSpeak. There are many words and phrases that have special meaning in publishing. There are also abbreviations that stand for associations important to the life of authors and editors. Most first-time authors, to hide their newness to the publishing fraternity, hide their lack of knowledge of these special terms. Now you can be an insider, too.

AA   Authors Alterations. Changes that the author makes after the galley proofs are provided by the publisher. Most publisher-author contracts stipulate a penalty if the author's changes are excessive.

AAP   Association of American Publishers. The industry association of book publishers, primarily the larger publishers. Smaller publishers are organized into regional associations or by specialty.

AAUP   Association of American University Presses. The publishers associated with colleges and universities who publish both scholarly and popular trade books.

ABA   American Booksellers Association. The trade association

168

for the booksellers in the United States, providing a number of important services and training for bookseller members. The annual ABA Trade Exhibit is an excellent venue to see forthcoming books on display and to meet publishers and editors.

Advance   Moneys paid to the author prior to publication to be earned from royalties on sales. This same term is used by publishers to indicate the number of copies ordered prior to publication of a book (e.g., "We expected to advance 20,000 copies of the total printing of 40,000 copies.").

Agent   Hardly needs definition, but just in case, an independent representative of an author or other creative artist who sells the author's or artist's work to a third party and receives a commission on the sale, usually 10% to 15%. Some agents, especially those building a clientele, will represent unpublished authors. The term of the agency may extend over a number of works or on a single book basis. The author-agent agreement should be in writing.

ALA   American Library Association. An organization of librarians providing services to librarians. The ALA holds two excellent trade shows a year where publishers and others who sell to libraries meet.

Auction This is a process used by publishers (and authors on occasion) to ask other publishers to bid for rights, such as the paperback or book club rights. Bids are usually made by telephone in sequence, advancing by predetermined dollar amounts until only one publisher, the winner, remains. There is a high degree of trust between publishers, allowing this process to be the primary method of selling valuable rights.

Backlist   Titles that have been published previous to the current season and continue to sell sufficient copies to keep the book in print.

Book Club   Marketing organization that sells books to its members. The conventional view that Book-of-the-Month Club and the other widely advertised clubs are the primary customers for these rights is no longer valid. The Book-of-the-Month Club itself has diversified; there are many important specialized book clubs; and Scholastic Publishing has a major business in book clubs selling children's books to classrooms. Book clubs acquire the rights from the holder of the rights (usually the publisher), and pay an advance and royalty. The rights are often auctioned.

CD-ROM   Compact disc-read only memory. A compact disc on which a program has been recorded that usually stores a vast amount of text or text combined with other media, such as video clips, photographic images, and sound. The disc is similar in size and shape to an audio compact disc (CD), but can only be played in a compact disc player which is installed in a computer (called a CD-ROM drive). "Read only memory" means that you can't alter or add to the disc's contents.

College Store   A bookstore located on or near a college campus, serving the students and faculty (and sometimes the public). Some stores are owned by the university; others are operated under a lease from the university by private corporations that specialize in operating college bookstores.

Cooperative Advertising   Ads run by a bookseller in which part of the cost is paid by a publisher. This is an important means of getting stock into a bookstore and announcing the availability of the book to the public.

Copyediting   Careful review of a manuscript prior to publication by an expert in grammar, punctuation, sentence structure, and clarity. This is a function performed by the publisher at his expense. The results of copyediting are furnished to the author for review and acceptance.

Copyright   This is a property right possessed by the author once the work is fixed in any tangible form (e.g., typed, handwritten, filmed, etc.). Copyright does not protect "ideas," only the author's particular expression of those ideas. Under the present law, copyright is not lost if notice ("c" in a circle [©]) is omitted. Registration with the Copyright Office is only required if you sue for infringement. However, authors are well advised to take those steps to identify their ownership. The author owns a "bundle of rights" under copyright. These rights may be conveyed separately. If the rights granted are exclusive, the grant must be in writing. The term of the copyright is the life of the author plus fifty years. However, even if the grant to the publisher is for the full term of the copyright, the author has a right to terminate any license after thirty-five years. For further information write the Register of Copyrights, United States Copyright Office, Library of Congress, Washington, DC 20559.

El-Hi   The educational market covering elementary grades (kindergarten to grade eight) and high school (grades nine through twelve).

Fair Use   The right, under Section 107 of the Copyright Act, to use materials, published or unpublished, in a carefully restricted manner without permission of the copyright holder. Use of another's copyrighted material in the author's work, without permission, is not a decision an author should take without legal advice.

Foreign Rights   The rights owned by the author, which can be conveyed to the publisher in writing, to publish her book outside the United States, either on her own or through a license with a foreign publisher.

Frankfurt Book Fair   The largest international book fair in the world, attracting publishers from many countries; held in Frankfurt am Main, Germany, usually the first week in October each year.

Galleys   Refers to the first proofs of typeset materials and are the first time a manuscript appears set in type. Formerly, the galleys were long sheets on which two or three pages would appear; now most galleys appear on 8½ x 11-inch paper. In other instances, galleys are bound, usually uncorrected, and appear in actual page size. Unbound galleys are used for copyediting; bound galleys are used for advance reading by those who need to read the book far ahead of publication (reviewers, important buyers) in order to support its publication.

Guarantee   Normally used as an advance guarantee, which means that the advance on royalties is paid without any recourse on the part of the publisher as long as the publisher accepts the book for publication. Sometimes included in a contract as "non-recoverable advance."

Imprint   The name of a publisher (or its division or subsidiary) use to identify the books he publishes; normally shown on the spine of the book, the jacket, and title page.

Jacket   Designed paper cover over a bound book, sometimes referred to as a dust jacket. The author is often consulted by the publisher on the jacket design since it is a primary selling tool for the book at point of sale.

Juvenile   A shorthand way of referring to a book written for children (e.g., juvenile books).

List   The books published by a publisher that are currently in print. When used as the publisher's list, it refers to the catalog of the publisher.

Literary Agent   *See* Agent.

LMP *Literary Market Place.* The annual directory of publishers and the entire industry, published by R. R. Bowker. If you are unfamiliar with this book, go to your public library reference section and study it. It is an invaluable tool for someone who wishes to be her own agent. See Appendix B for more information as to content and use.

Logo Trademark or indicia used by the publisher to identify his company.

Mail Order Usually associated with direct-mail sales. Certain books can be sold directly to the buyer through advertisements offering the book, or through direct-mail letters addressed to potential buyers. Books are then shipped through the mail.

Mass Market There are an estimated one hundred thousand retail stores in which books are sold that are not traditional bookstores (some examples are supermarkets, drugstores, and warehouse outlets) and this market is defined as the mass market. Previously, mass market outlets sold only paperbacks and lower priced children's books. Not so today. However, rack-sized paperbacks are often referred to as mass market paperbacks to distinguish them from the trade paperbacks generally sold only in bookstores.

MultiMedia Refers to products in which print, illustration, sound, and film are mixed, generally for utilization in a computer. (See also CD-ROM.)

Option A commitment that the current publisher can acquire a subsequent work of an author prior to that work being made available to competing publishers. Term may also apply to licenses. For instance, a primary publisher commits to a secondary publisher (who has licensed certain rights to an author's work) that he will be given first opportunity to obtain the same rights to a subsequent work before it is offered to competing publishers.

OP (Out of Print)   Refers to those books that are out of print and no longer available in the publisher's stock.

Paperback   A book bound with a paper cover (usually illustrated), as opposed to a book which has a hard, board binding. See also mass market.

Permission   The right to use previously published or as yet unpublished material in a work with suitable acknowledgment to the author granting the permission. The permission to use the material is usually obtained from the Permissions Department of the originating publisher. A fee may be required. To facilitate clearances of material primarily in journals, there is a Copyright Clearance Center from which permissions can be sought.

Professional Books   Created primarily for professionals, such as doctors, nurses, engineers.

Publicity   An activity other than space and cooperating advertising, undertaken by a publisher to make the public aware of an author's book. This includes such measures as author tours, book signings, posters, review copy mailings, catalogs, etc.

PW   *Publishers Weekly*, the primary weekly industry trade publication. This is essential reading for authors and especially those authors who wish to be their own agent. Available in most public libraries.

Religious Books   Traditionally referred to Bibles, prayer books, hymnals, testaments, and other sacred books. Recently the definition has been expanded to include inspirational books with religious underpinnings and other books that guide readers in the exploration and practice of many of the world's religions and philosophies.

Remainders   Books that the publisher cannot sell at the full price through normal channels that are offered, as long as the stock remains, to the retailers at a sharply lower price, and which the retailer offers to the public at a fraction of the regular selling price. In some instances, these so-called remainder books are created to provide the consumer a good value. In other instances, a book unsuccessful at the full price finds a new and continuing market at the lower price and stays in print for a longer period of time as a remainder.

Reprint   A new printing of the book by the original publisher or a printing of the book by a licensed publisher. In the first instance, the publisher watches the sales data, and before the supply of the book is exhausted, orders a reprint using the original production materials stored at the printer. In the second instance, the original publisher feels that he has exhausted all efforts to sell to his market and finds another publisher who specializes in reprinting previously published books. Printing technology now makes it possible to print as few as fifty copies economically and to price them so a reader may acquire them. This is useful for an author to know so she can encourage a publisher to keep her book available to the public.

Reserve   An accounting procedure used by publishers to provide for a future expense contemplated by the publisher. A returns reserve is an estimate of the expense to be incurred when books are returned.

Returns   Books that are unsold and returned by the retailer or wholesaler to the publisher. Some booksellers buy books on a non-returnable basis and are given a price incentive, but essentially all books are returnable at the option of the bookseller, within some general standards set by the publisher. Alfred Knopf, one of the great men in publishing, disparagingly said the policy was typified by the statement, "Gone today and here tomorrow." The author should not be concerned because the publisher withholds royalty payments (a "return reserve") to offset potential returns. Ultimately, after all the returns are in, the author receives the money due her in a final accounting.

Review Copy   Free copies sent to established book reviewers for newspapers and magazines. The publisher has a list of reviewers and is hopeful that the receipt of a copy will generate interest. Reviews in newspapers and periodicals are an essential part of the promotion of a book.

Royalties   The amount received by an author based upon sales of her book. Royalties are expressed in a percentage of the retail price (the suggested price printed on the jacket of the book). Sometimes, royalties are based upon the net receipts (the price of the book as shown in a publisher's catalog less the bookstore's discount, generally 40-45%) or, in the case of non-bookstore sales, a percentage of the publisher's receipts (e.g., special sales where they may be 10% of the net received). Royalties that are earned by sales are offset against the advance payment. Earned royalties must surpass the advance before the author receives additional royalty payments.

Scholarly Books   A broad designation to cover books in highly specialized areas of knowledge that are designed essentially for a limited market, although some books of note move over to the trade list occasionally.

Serialization   Magazines and newspapers often condense a book or select important sections of a book and publish them. If the magazine or newspaper is allowed to do this prior to publication of the book, it is first serialization; if serialization appears after the book has been released, it is second serialization. This is an important distinction, because in the former case the author receives 85–90% of the income; in the latter case, the income is usually shared equally.

Slush Pile   See *Unsolicited Manuscript.*

Software   The reinterpretation of the essence of the book, possibly combined with other material supplied by the software developer, to create a disc or CD-ROM for use in a computer.

Space Advertising   Paid ads placed by the publisher in newspapers and magazines promoting the book.

Special Sales   Sales of the book made by the publisher to accounts outside of bookstores, often in large quantities at low prices and with a lower royalty to the author.

Subscription Reference Books   Multi-volume encyclopedias or specialized reference books marketed by door-to-door salesmen or by direct-mail offers. Customers agree to buy the entire set.

Subsidiary Rights   Rights derived from the literary work and owned by the author (other than the primary right to publish the literary work). For example, if the author conveys only hardcover publication rights in the English language to the U.S. and Canada, all other rights such as translation, foreign sales, paperback, book club publication, etc., are subsidiary rights.

Textbooks   Books created by publishers specializing in the educational market for adoption for use in schools. Sales are made directly to school districts.

Title Page   The page at the beginning of the book, normally on the right side, which sets forth the title, the author, and publisher.

The reverse side of the title page, the copyright page, normally contains the copyright notice and other essential information to assist the reader in reaching the publisher if necessary.

Trade Books   Books created primarily for the general reader to be sold to the public through bookstores.

Trade Discount   The percentage that the publisher will reduce the price to provide a margin for the trade seller of the book. The schedules of trade discounts vary by publishers and are further complicated by incentives to buy on a nonreturnable basis.

Trade Paperback   Normally a softcover reprint of a hardcover trade book in approximately the same size as the trade book (often printed from the same plates) that is sold at a lower price in a retail bookstore because it has a soft cover.

University Press   A publishing firm sponsored by a university. In all respects, this entity is like other publishers, except for the character of the books published, which is generally scholarly.

Unsolicited Manuscript   Manuscript submitted to the publisher directly by the author (not through an agent) without invitation from the publisher. Sometimes referred to as the Slush Pile or manuscripts received "over the transom."

Vanity Publishing   Publication done by a publisher who requires that the author pay for all the costs of publication and distribution as well as "overhead costs." If the prospects for publication by a conventional publisher are remote, the author is better advised to self-publish rather than use a vanity publisher. There are a number of excellent books on self-publishing, and assistance is available from organizations that are involved in self-publishing.

How to Use
Literary Market Place
to Find Your Publisher
and Editor

■ Your single most important reference source to locate the publishers to whom you should send your proposal and the name of the editor to whom the proposal should be addressed is *Literary Market Place*, referred to by those in the know as *LMP.* It also can serve many other useful purposes.

The thick volume has more than seventeen hundred pages, is published annually by R. R. Bowker, and is available at most public libraries. Since book publishing seems to be in constant motion with mergers and acquisitions, and editors often move from one house to another, other trade sources such as *Publishers Weekly* should be used to update information in *LMP* between annual editions. If updating the information through *Publishers Weekly* (also published by R. R. Bowker) is not possible, a telephone call to the publisher and editor you have chosen will enable you to check the accuracy of the information essential to you. (The entries from LMP which follow are for illustration only and may be out of date. Do not use this information to locate a publisher or editor.)

You will find these examples of sections of *LMP* useful to you:

The List of U.S. Book Publishers

This is an alphabetical list of all the small, midsized, and large publishers in the United States. This is essential information. Below are samples of what you will find, and how to use them.

Where to Send Your Manuscript

Publisher

Directory information provides you with the address and telephone number of whom to send your adult hardcover manuscript.

Henry Holt & Co Inc
115 W 18 St., New York NY 10011
SAN: 200-2108
Tel: 212-886-9200; 800-488-5233
FAX: 212-633-0748
Warehouse: 4375 W 1980 S,
Salt Lake City, UT 84101

This personnel information provides you with a choice. Since the editor-in-chief would rarely be a first reader, any of the other editors might be chosen but your best bet is the senior editor.

Pres & Publisher: Bruno A. Quinson
VP, Cont: Charles H Fischer III
VP, Sales & Mktg: Gregory Hamlin
VP, & Ed-in-Chief Adult Books:
    William Strachan
VP & Dir, Subs Rts: Wendy Sherman
VP, Adult Books: John Macrae III
Exec Ed: Marian Wood
Eds-at-Large: Elizabeth Crossman;
    Cynthia Vartan
Edit Dir, Books: Kenneth Wright
    Sr Ed: Allen Peacock

Owl Books is a paperback imprint, and if you have a likely subject, which you would discover after checking the Owl catalog, you would submit your manuscript to the editorial director.

Ed, Owl Books: Theresa Burns
Ed-in-Chief, Books for Young Readers:
    Brenda Bowen
Art Dir, Books for Young Readers:
    Maryann Leffingwell
Foreign & Juv Book Rts: Janette Carrier

Juvenile Books: Holt has an excellent line of children's books. The editors to whom you should send your manuscript are listed in this entry.

Publicity Dir: Lottchen Shivers
Mktg Dir, Books for Young Readers:
    Carol Roeder
Adv & Prom Mgr: Joanna Dowey
Sales Dir: Mark Levine
Dir, Spec Mkt: Judith Sisko
Prodn Dir: Barbara Miller
Art Dir: Raquel Jaramillo
Dir, Legal affairs: Muriel Caplan
Assoc Ed, Ref Books: Mary Kay Linge
Sr Ed, Books for Young Readers:
    Marc Aronson
Ed, Books for Young Readers:
    Laura Godwin
Dist for Anlon; DLM Inc; Miller
    Heiman Inc; Slack Inc; Viceroy Press

This listing of the number of titles published each year is a very good index to the current size. Publishers who issue 100-200 new books each year are ideal targets for submission. They are not too large to be deluged with submissions. The size of the backlist and the date founded is a sign, but not a guarantee, of stability.

Directories, reference, childrens books.
1992: 300 titles. In print: 1000 titles.
Founded 1866
ISBN Prefix(es): 0-08050
Adv Agency: Denhard & Stewart
Imprints: Don Hutter Books; John
    Maccrae Books; Mill Martin Jr Books
Subsidiaries: Management Information
    Sources Inc
Divisions: Twenty-First Century Books
Foreign Reps: Fitheny & Whiteside
    (Canada)
Foreign Rts: A/S Bookman
    Literary Agency
    (Denmark, Finland, Iceland,
    Norway); Agenzia Letteraria
    Internazionale (Italy); Agencia
    Literaria Balcells, Mello e Souza, Riff
    (Brazil, Portugal, Spain, South
    America); International Literatuur
    Bureau B V (Holland); Japan UNI
    Agency Inc (Japan); Agence Michelle
    Lapautre (France); Judy Martin (UK,

Australia); GPA Gerd Plessl Agentur (Eastern Europe, Greece); Nurcihan Kesim (Turkey); Paul & Peter Fritz Agency (Germany); Rogan I Pikarski Ltd Literary Agent (Israel)

You should follow this process of reviewing a listing for all except the major publishers. For the major publishers you will find a master listing, which usually contains the names of corporate officers, and then you should seek out the subordinate listings that show the editors.

Finding Your Way around the Conglomerates

Bantam Doubleday Dell Publishing Company Inc. is the combination of three major publishers under one owner, Bertelsmann, a German publisher, which owns publishers around the world. To find the market for your book, you must find each of the independent publishing entities within the conglomerate and analyze it as you did in the case of Holt. Keep in mind that for all publishing conglomerates, you must use the following process. Here is the example of a corporate directory:

Where to Send Your Manuscript

This listing is not useful for your purpose; it identifies the executives. Skip over them to get to the individual corporate listings.

Publisher

Corporate Entity

Bantam Doubleday Dell Publishing
   Company Inc
Affil of Bertelsmann
666 Fifth Ave, New York, NY 10103
Tel: 212-765-6500; 800-223-6834
Telex: 7608009 FAX: 212-765-3869
Chmn: Bernhard von Minckwitz
Pres & CEO: Jack Hoeft
Pres, Sales & Mktg: Stephen Weitzen
Group Sr VP, Pres & Publisher, Bantam
   Books: Irwyn Applebaum
Group Sr VP, Pres & Publisher, Dell
   Publishing & Bantam Doubleday
Dell Books for Young Readers:
   Carole Baron
Group Sr VIP, Pres & Publisher,
   Linda Grey Books: Linda Grey
Group Sr VP, Pres & Publisher,
   Intl Div: Alun Davies
Exec VP & CEO: Peter Olson
Group Sr VP: John Choi
Group Sr VP & Dir, PR:
   Stuart Applebaum
Exec VP & Chief Admin Officer:
   William Wright
Sr VP & Gen Counsel:
   Harriette Dorsen
Group VP & Corp Cont:
   Jon de Beaumont
Sr VP, Human Resources: Joe Crean
VP, Personnel: Terry Gioia
VP, Fulfillment: Phyllis Mandel
See Bantam Books; Doubleday;
   Dell Publishing
BISG member.

Note address, which in this instance is the same as the corporate address.

Bantam Entity

‡§Bantam
Div of Bantam Doubleday Dell
   Publishing Group Inc
666 Fifth Ave, New York, NY 10103
Tel: 212-765-6500; 800-223-6835
Telex: 7608009
Cable: BANTAMBOOK NY
FAX: 212-765-3869
Shipping: 414 E Golf Dr, Des Plaines,
   IL 60016
Pres & Publisher: Linda Grey

There is only one name listed for adult hardcover, trade, and paperback books. This is not very helpful—but it is the only entry you have. It is still better to address your material to a specific editor. He will usually pass it on to the correct person.

VP & Publisher, Adult Hardcover &
   Trade
Paperback Books: Jeff Stone
VP & Publisher, Bantam Spectra,
   Foundation
Dir, Publicity: Carol Fass
Publicity Mgr, Author Prom:
   Diane Ekeblad
Publicity Mgr, Press Rels:
   Beverly Robinson
Publicity Mgr, West Coast: Liz William
Dir, Educ: Tamu Aljuwani
VP & Exec Man Ed: Betsy Elias
Man Ed, Trade: Stephen McNabb
VP & Dir, Prodn Opers:
   George Davidson
Sr VP & Dir, Adv & Prom: Marcia Blitz
VP & Exec Art Dir: Charles Bjorklund
Prodn Mgr: Janice Waldman
VP & Art Dir: Don Munson
VP & Dir, Creative Devt: Risa Kessler
Sr VP & Dir, Busn Opers:
   Gilbert Perlman
Sr VP & Dir, Sales: Stephen Black
VP & Dir, Field Sales: John Conti
Natl Accts Mgr: Michael Murphy
Dir, Wholesale Sales: Tim De Young
Dir, Subs Rts: Teri Henry
VP & Mgr, Intl Sales: Tom Flynn

Some modest assistance in defining books published. It is far better to send for catalogs.

Dist. for Warner Books
General fiction & nonfiction hardcover; trade & mass market paperbacks; science fiction.
1990: 633 titles. In print: 5000 titles
Founded 1952
ISBN Prefix(es): 0-345 (Ballantine, Del Rey);
0-449 (Fawcett); 0-804 (Ivy)

Other imprints—some of which are major. Ask for catalogs for these imprints.

Imprints: Ballantine Books; Ballantine/ Available Press; Del Rey Books; Fawcett Columbine; Fawcett Crest; Fawcett Gold Medal; Fawcett Juniper; Fawcett Premier; House of Collectibles; Ivy Books

Dell Publishing—separate alphabetically under "D"

‡§Dell Publishing
Div of Bantam Doubleday Dell Publishing Group Inc
666 Fifth Ave, New York NY 10103
SAN: 201-0097
Tel: 212-765-6500; 800-223-6834
Telex: 23-8781 DELL UR
Cable: DELL PUB FAX: 212-492-9698
Shipping: 30 E Oakton Ave, Des Plaines, IL 60016

Once again the corporate listing is not useful to you. Skip to the editorial department.

Pres & Publisher: Carole Baron
Pres, Sales & Mktg: Stephen Weitzen
VP, Assoc Publisher: Isabel Geffner
VP & Dir, Sales Admin: Marty McGrath
VP Sales, Retail: Jim Chandler
VP Sales, Wholesale: George Harris
VP Sales, Jobber: David Lappin
VP Sales, Specialty Mkts: Mike Pegan
VP, Sales & Mktg: Reed Boyd
Dir, Independent Retail Sales: Susan Peterson
VP & Dir, Mktg: Paul Fedorko
Mktg Dir, Retail: Richard Hunt
Mktg Dir, Wholesale: Paul Stafford

Dir, Retail Chains: Jay Melton
Mktg Dir, Jobber: Cynthia Kleinman
Dir Mktg, Adult Hardcover & Trade:
    Carol Lappin
Mktg Mgr, Adult Hardcover & Trade:
    Beth Barry
Creative Dir, Adv & Prom: David Vozar
Dir, Adv & Prom: Pam Ataway
VP & Art Dir, Covers:
    Gerald Counihan
VP, Exec Dir Publicity: Roger Bilheimer
Dir, Publicity: Laurence Hughes
Assoc Dir, Publicity: Judy Westerman
VP & Ed-in-chief: Leslie Schnur
Assoc Publisher, Romance Fiction:
Damaris Rowland
Exec Ed: Cynthia White
Exec Ed: Laurel Books & Dell Trade
Pbk: Trish Todd

Based solely on the listing, the people listed as senior editors are most likely the best people to send your manuscript to. However, there are a number of imprints—Laurel, Trade Paperbacks, and Dell Books for Young Readers—and you should make sure you are approaching the appropriate editor. Managing editors are generally a less desirable contact because they have significant administrative duties and they, in general, do not read manuscripts. When these are the only names provided, send your material to the managing editor, who might refer it to the appropriate editor for reading.

Sr Eds: Jackie Cantor; Tina Miskow;
    Jeanne Cavelos
Man Ed, Dell Books: Sandi Borger
Eds: Mitch Horowitz; Jill Lamar;
    E J McCarthy
Copy Chief: Elizabeth Kantor
Mgr, Contracts: Dorothy Boyajy
Dir, Continuity Sales: John Rutledge
Dir, Premium Mktg: Bob Hirsch
Dir, Specialty Mkts: Janet Cooke
Dir, Spec Sales: Stephen Mudgett
Sr VP & Dir, Direct Response:
    Sally Wood
VP, Continuity & Collections:
    Marc Jacob
Sr VP & Chief Admin Officer:
    William Wright
VP, Prodn & Purch: Rusty Hannon
VP, Fulfillment: Phyllis Mandel
Assoc Gen counsel: Suzanne Telsey
    Agency (Hebrew); Lennart Sane

Doubleday—separate alphabetically under "D"

‡§Doubleday
Div of Bantam Doubleday Dell
Publishing Group Inc
666 Fifth Ave, New York, NY 10103
Tel: 212-765-6500; 800-223-6834
Telex: 23-7019
Cable: DOUBDAY FAX: 212-492-9700
   (correspondence); 212-492-9862
   (orders)
Shipping: 30 E Oakton Ave,
   Des Plaines, IL 60016

These are the senior editorial executives—not useful as a source for unsolicited manuscripts.

Pres & Publisher: Stephen Rubin
Pres, Sales & Mktg: Stephen Weitzen
VP & Deputy Publisher: William Barry
VP & Ed-in-chief: David Gernert

Nan A. Talese Books is an example of a specialized imprint and is not a good place to send an unsolicited manuscript.

Sr VP, Ed Dir & Publisher of Nan A
   Talese Books: Nan A Talese
Dir, Subs Rts: Carol Lazare
VP, Sales Admin: Marty McGrath
VP Sales, Special Mkts: Michael Pegan
VP, Sales, Jobber: David Lappin
Marketing Dir, Jobber:
   Cynthia Kleinman
VP, Sales, Retail: Jim Chandler
Dir, Independent Retail Sales:
   Susan Peterson
Retail Sales Mktg Dir: Richard Hunt
Mktg Dir, Wholesale: Paul Stafford
VP, Sales & Mktg: Jacqueline Everly
VP & Dir, Creative Servs: Jack Looney
VP & Creative Dir: Whitney Cookman
VP & Deputy Gen Counsel:
   Kathy Trager
VP & Publisher, Anchor Books: Martha
   Levin

These editors are at a level that might be helpful.

Dir, Religious Publishing:
   Thomas Cahill
Sr Edit Con: Nancy Nicholas

Sr VP & Ed-at-Large: Herman Gollob
VP & Exec Ed, Currency Books:
    Harriet Rubin

Send to these senior editors (by category when available). When in doubt, call and ask the editorial assistant, who will answer the telephone, for the name of the editor working in your genre.

Exec Ed: Deborah Futter
Sr Eds: Charles Conrad; Joel Fishman;
Judith Kern; Jacqueline Onassis
Sr ed, DD Westerns: Tom Dupree
VP, Assoc Publishers & Exec Man Ed:
    Michele Martin
Sr Art Dir: Julie Duquet
Art Dir: Peter Kruzan
Cont: Donald Echart
Contracts: Paula Breen
Copyrights & Perms: Carol
Christiansen
Assoc Mktg Dir: John Pitts;
    Jayne Schorn
Dir, Adv & Proms: Deborah Koenig
VP, Assoc Publisher & Exec Dir,
Publicity: Marly Russoff
Dir, Publicity: Ellen Archer
Publicity Mgrs: Ginger Barton; Nina
    Mehta
Publicists: Marian Brown; Amy Baron
Sr Publicist: Paola Rana
Dir, Subs Rts Contracts: Judith Hansen
Assoc Dir, Subs Rts: Kevin Lang
Dir, Natl Accts: Linda Stormes
Mgr, Sales Admin: Lee Swenka
Dir, Continuity Programs:
    John Rutledge

This information is helpful because it describes the areas in which Doubleday publishes. However, nothing replaces getting catalogs, visiting a bookstore, or attending a trade show where you can see the

Dist by Main Street/Back List
Hardcover & paperback books for the general & special interest markets, including fiction, nonfiction, mysteries, romance, Westerns, science, science fiction, religion, bibles, biography, business, history & reference.

publisher's display and talk to editors and salespersons.

1992: 350 titles. In print: 1200 titles.
Founded 1987
ISBN Prefix(s): 0-385

Indices

LMP has three indices that are helpful. Publishers are organized:

1. Geographically by state.

2. By type of publication.

Under each heading, there is a one line listing or the publisher's name. To find more detailed information concerning the publisher, you must go back to the alphabetical listing in the front of the book.

Typical listings are: Association Presses, Audio Cassettes, A.V. Materials, Bibliographies, Braille Books, Data Bases, and Dictionaries & Encyclopedias.

3. By subject.

Typical entries are: Accounting, Advertising, Aeronautics, and Aviation.

The difficulty with these listings is that there are so many publishers listed in each category. A significant amount of work is required to find the most desirable publishers in each category to whom to submit your work.

Small Presses

There is a limited listing of small presses which might be helpful when your book is designed for a limited, specific market. There is a more complete listing available from the Small Press Center at 20 West 44th Street, New York, NY 10036; Tel: 212-764-7021; FAX: 212-354-5365.

Literary Agents

This is an excellent listing, albeit somewhat discouraging. In almost every instance, the agents' listings say, "No unsolicited mss, query first." There are additional directories of agents available, but this one is extensive and useful.

Calendar of Book Trade and Professional Events

This is a listing by month of events, many of which are useful for the first-time author. Major events such as the American Booksellers Association and the American Library Association trade exhibits are listed with the current venues and specific dates. The Regional Book Exhibits are listed, as well as meetings for specialists such as the Garden Writers Association of America. This is an extremely valuable listing.

Writers Conferences and Workshops

Many of the writers conferences, with information as to the sponsorship, the dates held, and the location appear in this listing. The Guide to Writers Conferences can be ordered from Show Guides, 625 Beltome Way, Suite 1406, Coral Gables, FL 33134, $18.95, is a better directory with more conferences shown and more complete information.

Yellow Pages

You can use the yellow pages to find the name, address, telephone number, and fax number of the editors. This is a useful index once you know the name of the individual. It does not meet your primary need of identifying the editor to whom you should send your book. The main directory of publishers does this.

Since finding the *right publisher* and the *right editor* are crucial to the ultimate success of your endeavor, becoming familiar with *LMP* is essential. Spend an hour or more just getting to know the directory; it is extensive and is designed for use by publishers and booksellers, but the sections discussed above can be extremely useful to you as well.

While *LMP, Publishers Weekly,* and other printed information is valuable, even more important is your own Rolodex, or whatever device you use to store names, addresses, and telephone and fax numbers. Using *LMP* as a base, start your own Rolodex and add to the identifying information all the seemingly unimportant, but actually very important, information, such as the name of the editorial assistant or secretary and her telephone number when you discover it, and any information that will make the editorial needs more focused, for example, "prefers mysteries with unusual detectives." The most important tool of any agent is his Rolodex. It will be your most valuable tool as well.

| A |
| P |
| P |
| E |
| N | # Best Bets—
The Publishers
Most Likely to
Read and Accept
Your Book |
| D |
| I |
| X |
| C |

■ The chances of having your book read is far better with a smaller publisher than the fifteen major publishers, with notable exceptions. Some major publishers still read unsolicited manuscripts and many read query letters. Even though the chances of having your book read and accepted are much lower, the large publishers should be on your target list. The purpose of Best Bets is to call your attention to the smaller publishers which you might otherwise have overlooked.

The selection of publishers is based chiefly on my personal experience, and there may be many other publishers who deserve to be here. I have included some notes about books they are likely to publish, where known. While my notes will be helpful you should send for a catalog or arrange to see their display at the annual ABA Trade Exhibit. These are trade publishers, most of whom publish in hardcover and trade paperback. Check the address in the current *LMP* before you submit material.

The abbreviations used to indicate the types of books they publish are:

F	fiction	C	computer instruction
NF	nonfiction	CREF	consumer reference
J	juvenile	H	humor

Addison-Wesley Publishing Company
One Jacob Way
Reading, MA 01867

NF, J, C

From time to time, AW books make the best-seller list. For example, *Iron John* by Robert Bly was, according to *PW*, the twelfth-best nonfiction title for 1991. This book sold almost 146,000 copies in 1990 (with a first printing of 30,000 copies) and almost 320,000 copies in 1991. It was on the best-seller list for fifty weeks and created the men's movement category in bookstores.

Adams Publishing
260 Center Street
Holbrook, MA 02343

F, H

One of the fastest-growing mid-sized trade publishers, with an emphasis on business and careers, self-improvement, women's studies, pets, parenting, cookbooks, sports, games, and humor. If your book is published by Adams you'll receive topnotch promotion and attention.

Algonquin Books of Chapel Hill
Box 2225
Chapel Hill, NC 27515

F, NF

A distinguished publisher (mainly of literary nonfiction and fiction) eager to find new talent. The standards are high and their list should be studied before submitting a pro-

posal. They are known for their willingness to respond to serious authors.

Andrews & McMeel
4900 Main Street
Kansas City, MO 64112

NF, H, CREF

One of the most creative of all publishers and, because of its calendar and humor line, bigger than you might think. Send for a catalog before submitting, because they have a special style of book with which they do superbly.

Arcade Publishing
141 Fifth Avenue
New York, NY 10010

NF, F, J

Owned by Jeannette and Richard Seaver, two experienced and very talented editor-publishers. Their list is small and their advances are low, but they select books carefully, edit them well, and have distribution through Little, Brown, so they reach all the bookstores. Send query or outstanding proposal.

August House
P.O. Box 3233
Little Rock, AR 72203

F, NF, H, J

A midsized press that specializes in American storytelling and folklore, fiction, cooking, humor, and regional titles. If you have an idea for a book with a southern slant, try this publisher.

Avery Publishing Group
120 Old Broadway
Garden City Park, NY 11040

NF

Solid nonfiction publisher in the areas of health, cookbooks, lifestyle, parenting, business, history, and others.

Barron's Educational Series
250 Wireless Boulevard
Hauppauge, NY 11788

NF, CREF, J, C

No longer a small or midsized publisher, they publish over 250 new books each year, most of them generated from ideas they provide to authors. Barron's started as an educational directory publisher but they are now a major factor in almost every bookstore, large or small.

Beacon Press
25 Beacon Street
Boston, MA 02108

NF, F

An excellent publisher for nonfiction books in the areas of religion and theology, current affairs, women's studies, and other, serious nonfiction areas.

Peter Bedrick Books
2112 Broadway
New York, NY 10023

NF, J

Peter Bedrick is a publisher who has developed an outstanding list of illustrated books that can be read by the adult and still be appreciated by a young reader. Most books are imported from abroad, but Peter Bedrick will acquire the occasional book that fits his publishing orientation, especially if the book is a heavily illustrated nonfiction book that can fit within or start a series.

Betterway Books
1507 Dana Avenue
Cincinnati, OH 45207

NF

A midsized publisher that specializes in the following nonfiction areas: homebuilding, business, self-help, automotive, parenting, and crafts.

Bonus Books
160 East Illinois Street
Chicago, IL 60611

NF

A midwestern publisher that started strongly in sports and has branched out into other areas, among them business, regional books, games and gambling, cookbooks, collectibles, diet and health, and family.

Thomas Bouregy & Co.
401 Lafayette Street
New York, NY 10003

F

A wonderful starting point for the first-time author who can write wholesome romance novels. The payments are modest but this is definitely a first step on the ladder. Send query letter and sample of writing.

Carol Publishing Group
600 Madison Avenue
New York, NY 10022

NF, F

The successor to one of the most personal of all American publishers, Lyle Stuart. The books currently being published are not as sensuous or flamboyant as were the prior owner's. The nonfiction work must have wide consumer appeal.

Carroll & Graf Publishers
260 Fifth Avenue
New York, NY 10001

F, NF

Two outstanding editor-publishers have created a house that publishes about 150 titles a year in hardcover and paperback.

Celestial Arts
see Ten Speed Press

Specializes in popular psychology, self-help, health, and healing; was acquired by Ten Speed Press and is an excellent, responsive publisher for the right book.

Chelsea House Publishers
300 Park Avenue South
New York, NY 10010

NF, J, CREF

A good buyer for nonfiction (history, reference, and literary criticism), and serious juvenile books, especially in the multicultural area.

Children's Press
5440 N. Cumberland Avenue
Chicago, IL 60656

J

A major publisher of heavily illustrated juvenile books, especially those that can be used to supplement classroom teaching and in libraries.

Chilton Enterprises
201 King of Prussia Road
Radnor, PA 19089

CREF

One of the largest publishers of technical books, automotive books for the consumer and repair professional, and other general consumer reference books.

Chronicle Books
275 Fifth Avenue
San Francisco, CA 94103

F, NJ, J

Having built this list from regional titles into a world-class publishing operation, this is a market for guide books, fine arts, cookbooks, design, photography, and more recently, illustrated children's books, gift books, fiction, stationery products, and calendars. Just published a first novel and have another forthcoming.

Chronimed Publishing
13911 Ridgedale Drive
Suite 250
Minneapolis, MN 55343

NF

Health is the all-encompassing subject here, with "niche" books on self-help, diet, fitness, and illness.

Contemporary Books
Two Prudential Plaza
Chicago, IL 60601

F, NF

With the additional investment from the *Chicago Tribune*, its present owner, this successful publisher should grow significantly. This company has a strong nonfiction orientation, and the author should request a catalog before submitting her work.

The Continuum Publishing Group
370 Lexington Avenue
New York, NY 10017

F, NF

This is a serious publisher, especially interested in scholarly and professional books for the trade market. They publish in the fields of literature and criticism, psychology and social thought, performing arts, and women's studies.

The Countryman Press
Box 175
Woodstock, VT 05091

F, NF

Essentially a publisher specializing in books about New England, this publisher will also consider books on skiing, travel, nature, walking, and related outdoor subjects.

DAW Books Inc.
375 Hudson Street
New York, NY 10014

F

Science fiction, fantasy, and horror only. The best and most sophisticated is what attracts the editors at this excellent small publisher, now affiliated with Penguin Books.

Enslow Publishers
Box 777
Bloy Street and Ramsey Avenue
Hillside, NJ 07205

J

Juvenile and young adult titles are published by this house under the direction of a family with a long history of successful publishing of juvenile books, primarily in the school and library market.

M. Evans & Company
216 East 49th Street
New York, NY 10017

F, NF, J

This publisher will accept commercial nonfiction and fiction in several areas, including romances and westerns as well as juveniles.

Facts on File
460 Park Avenue South
New York, NY 10016

NF, CREF, J

One of the largest publishers of reference books, both for general and professional audiences. "Reference" in this case is a particularly broad subject; besides dictionaries, encyclopedias, and atlases, they publish popular titles in the following areas: popular culture, business, current affairs, history, law, health, young adult, science, nature, sports, travel, and just about any other subject you can think of.

Farrar, Straus & Giroux
19 Union Square West
New York, NY 10003

F, NF, J

A distinguished publishing house. The books it publishes are at the top of the quality scale in every area. They will only accept extraordinary books. Try a query letter first.

Donald I. Fine, Inc.
19 West 21st Street
New York, NY 10010

F, NF

Donald Fine is the best judge of commercial fiction in publishing. His house exemplifies his taste and shows his ability to edit new authors. He discovered and nurtured Ken Follett until the money required to hold him was too large.

Fulcrum Publishing
350 Indiana Street
Suite 350
Golden, CO 80401

NF

A relatively new publisher who is steadily building up a solid backlist in the areas of nature, environmental issues, self-help, parenting, gardening, and travel. The general outlook of this house reflects its location.

Globe Pequot Press
6 Business Park Road
Old Saybrook, CT 06475

NF

Publishes a wide variety of nature, business, Americana, how-to, gardening, cooking, and other nonfiction categories.

David R. Godine, Publisher
Horticultural Hall
300 Massachusetts Avenue
Boston, MA 02115

F, NF, J

Typical of the personal publisher, David Godine and his staff carefully select books of high quality and relevance. Serious but lively nonfiction and well-written juveniles are a hallmark of this firm. Send for a catalog before submitting.

Grove/Atlantic Monthly
841 Broadway
New York, NY 10003

F, NF

A distinguished publisher, now better than ever under new management. Their list is wide-ranging, from belles lettres and poetry to cookbooks. They only publish about twenty-four books a year so they are very, very selective.

Gulf Publishing Company
Box 2608
Houston, TX 77252-2608

NF, CREF

Midsized publisher of recreation, business, regional (Texas/ Southwest), cookbooks, gardening, and engineering.

Harlequin Books
300 E. 42nd Street
New York, NY 10017

F

The world's largest publisher of romance fiction is still seeking authors who can write their kind of book with style.

The Harvard Common Press
535 Albany Street
Boston, MA 02118

NF

This is a good bet for a book on parenting and family matters. Small but sincere.

Hippocrene Books
171 Madison Avenue
New York, NY 10016

NF

Specialized nonfiction: history, military science, music, travel, Judaica.

Holmes & Meier
East Building
160 Broadway
New York, NY 10038

NF

A small publisher with a distinguished backlist in social sciences, humanities, political science, history, Judaica.

Henry Holt & Company
115 W. 18th Street
New York, NY 10011

F, NF, J, CREF, C

This is a modest-sized publisher that has grown so that now it publishes one of the major mystery writers, Sue Grafton, notable children's authors, computer books, dictionaries, and reference books. Well managed, well financed, and staffed with talented editors.

Hyperion
114 Fifth Avenue
New York, NY 10011

F, NF, J

Started as a division of Disney Book Publishing in 1992, publishing over one hundred new books a year, this is a well-financed start-up in need of the highest-quality general fiction, nonfiction, and children's books (Hyperion Books for Children at the same address).

Larousse Kingfisher Chambers
95 Madison Avenue
New York, NY 10016

J

London-based company which may be, for the right juvenile book or series, a good bet. The publisher prefers illustrated children's reference works, especially if these books can be developed into a series.

Leisure Books
276 Fifth Avenue
New York, NY 10001

F, NF

This is a mass market publisher that builds its list with original fiction in romance, westerns, mystery, and horror.

Lerner Publications Company
241 First Avenue North
Minneapolis, MN 55401

F, NF, J

Publishes largely in the juvenile field in science, history, sports, and some fiction, for the school and library as well as trade market.

Lyons & Burford Publishers
31 West 21 Street
New York, NY 10010

NF

Quality publisher primarily in the field of outdoor sports, natural history, and art.

McFarland & Company
Box 611
Jefferson, NC 28640

NF, CREF

Publishes almost exclusively reference works for library sales, but the list is surprisingly engaging; several books from each list are picked up by trade paperback houses for reprint.

Mercury House
201 Filbert Street
Suite 400
San Francisco, CA 94133

F, NF

This house seeks the highest quality fiction and nonfiction, especially in the areas of history, arts, communication, entertainment, environment, and biography.

Millbrook Press
2 Old New Milford Road
Brookfield, CT 06804

J

This is a strong publisher of juvenile books for classroom and library use, with some trade sales. Publishes over one hundred books a year.

Modern Publishing
155 East 55th Street
New York, NY 10022

NF, J, CREF

This publisher creates and publishes over one hundred books a year with strong emphasis on the juvenile and consumer reference titles.

John Muir Publications
Box 613
Santa Fe, NM 87504

NF, F, J

Originally a travel book publisher, now a growing juvenile publisher. The owners are open to new and exciting nonfiction ideas, specialized travel books, and unique juveniles.

National Textbook Company
4255 W. Touhy Avenue
Lincolnwood, IL 60646

NF, J

While this is a company that services the school market, they also have a strong presence in the trade with books in the areas of language, speech, mass communication, drama, business, marketing, and advertising.

Thomas Nelson
Nelson Place at Elm Hill Pike
Nashville, TN 37214

F, NF

Although one of the best Christian trade houses, Nelson publishes quite a few crossover books in the following areas: parenting, self-help, health, and even some adult and juvenile fiction. Sales to the Christian book market can be quite strong for the right book.

Nelson-Hall Publishers
111 N. Canal St.
Chicago, IL 60606

NF

General interest nonfiction in a variety of fields: self-help, history, travel, business, and others.

Newmarket Press
18 East 48th Street
New York, NY 10017

F, NF, CREF

This publisher, known for its movie tie-ins, also publishes highly visible books in consumer reference, self-help, and investment.

Open Court Publishing Company
315 Fifth Street
Peru, IL 61354

J

Primarily a publisher of elementary textbooks.

Paladin Press
Box 1307
Boulder, CO 80306

NF

A midsized publisher with a very specific scope: military and paramilitary, and all that encompasses (history, weaponry, martial arts and self-defense, espionage, survivalism, and even revenge).

Peachtree Publishers
494 Armour Circle NE
Atlanta, GA 30324

F, NJ, J

With only approximately twenty books published each year, they are selective, but a good bet.

Pelican Publishing Company
Box 3110
1101 Monroe Street
Gretna, LA 70053

F, NF, H

A regional house that specializes in cookbooks, humor, sports, inspirational, photography, juveniles, and travel, often with a regional slant. Fiction is infrequent.

Pineapple Press
Drawer 16008
Southside Station
Sarasota, FL 34239

F, NJ, J

If you have a book about Florida, the Southwest, or nature, this is indeed a Best Bet.

Presidio Press
505 B San Martin Drive
Suite 300
Novato, CA 94945

NF

A Best Bet for books on military history.

Price Stern Sloan
11150 Olympic Boulevard
Suite 650
Los Angeles, CA 90064

F, NF, J, H

Lots of humor, but also business, health, sports, automobiles, gardening, cookbooks, juveniles, and occasional fiction.

Prima Publishing
P.O. Box 1260
Rocklin, CA 95677

NF, C

Solid midsized publisher in the areas of business, cookbooks, self-help, health, lifestyle, computers, popular culture, travel, and sports.

Professional Publishing
1333 Burr Ridge Parkway
Burr Ridge, IL 60521

NF

The trade imprint for Irwin, the major college publisher. The books they publish are serious books for the business community in fields such as accounting, finance, communications, etc. The author should have the professional credentials to authenticate his book.

Prometheus Books
59 John Glenn Drive
Amherst, NY 14228

F, NF, J

Publishes books in a variety of areas: health, self-help, biography, philosophy, religion, politics, literature, reference, and occasional fiction.

Regnery Publishing
422 First Street SE
Suite 300
Washington, DC 20003

NF

A publisher of choice for authors of books that appeal to a politically conservative reading audience.

Rodale Press
33 E. Minor Street
Emmaus, PA 18098

NF

An outstanding publisher of books on nature, environment, organic gardening, health and nutrition, crafts and woodworking, and self-improvement.

Running Press
125 S 22nd Street
Philadelphia, PA 19103

NF, J

Stylishly designed books for house and home, art, science, and children.

Rutledge Hill Press
211 Seventh Avenue North
Nashville, TN 37219

NF

Young Nashville house that publishes quite a few titles each year in the following areas: popular culture, travel, cookbooks, history, health, and sports, often with a Southern twist.

Schiffer Publishing
1469 Morstein Road
West Chester, PA 19380

NF

Midsized trade publisher in the following areas: art and antiques, toys, hobbies, metaphysics, aviation, and automotive.

Gibbs Smith, Publisher
P.O. Box 667
Layton, UT 84041

F, NF, H, J

The main focus of this midsized publisher is the American West, whether it's reflected through fiction, general nonfiction, juveniles, cowboy poetry, or art. Also interested in architecture, cookbooks, and self-help.

Stackpole Books
P.O. Box 1831
Cameron & Kelker Streets
Harrisburg, PA 17105

NF

Longtime trade publisher in a few specific areas: the outdoors, adventure, woodworking, gardening, and military history.

St. Martin's Press
175 Fifth Avenue
New York, NY 10010

F, NF, J

A major publisher with a broad list of fiction and nonfiction in hardcover and paperback.

Steck-Vaughn Company
Box 26015
Austin, TX 78755

J

Sells into the school and library market with juvenile books, most heavily illustrated.

Sterling Publishing Company
387 Park Avenue South
New York, NY 10016

F, NF, J

Publishes a broad selection of nonfiction in almost every field of interest, and juvenile fiction.

Gareth Stevens
1555 N. River Center Drive
Milwaukee, WI 53212

J

Only juvenile books, especially those that are useful in classrooms and libraries.

The Summit Group
1227 West Magnolia
Fort Worth, TX 76104

NF, H

A fast-growing new publisher with a quick eye for the newest trends. Nicely designed books in the areas of humor, popular culture, trivia, juveniles, sports, and others.

Jeremy P. Tarcher
5858 Wilshire Boulevard
Los Angeles, CA 90036

NF

Highly selective publisher of professionally sound personal growth books with a psychological thrust.

Taylor Publishing
1550 West Mockingbird Lane
Dallas, TX 75235

NF

Solid midsized publisher of sports, health and family care, home improvement, fitness, gardening, self-help, and popular culture.

Ten Speed Press
Box 7123
Berkeley, CA 94707

NF

Accessible publisher of history, social sciences, business, cooking, gardening, recreation, hobbies, juvenile; prefers books of high quality which respond to strong marketing.

University Presses

For serious books, all university presses are Best Bets. For a complete directory with areas of publishing and names and addresses of editors write to: The Association of American University Presses, Inc., 585 Broadway, New York, NY 10012

Ventana Press
Box 2468
Chapel Hill, NC 27515

CREF

Excellent bet for computer books and software.

Walker and Company
435 Hudson
New York, NY 10014

F, NF

Trade publisher in the areas of health, sports, careers, self-help, parenting, personal investment, mysteries, and westerns.

John Wiley & Sons
605 Third Avenue
New York, NY 10158

NF, J, CREF

While largely a publisher of books on science and technology, it has a strong nonfiction trade list in personal finance, science, business, and juvenile reference.

Workman Publishing Company
708 Broadway
New York, NY 10003

NF

Noted for unusual nonfiction gift books and calendars.

Zebra Books
850 Third Avenue
New York, NY 10022

F, NF

Accessible publisher of hardcover, trade, and mass market paperback, with strong emphasis on romance, young adult, science fiction, and other genre fiction.

APPENDIX D
Manuscript Submission Record

■ Because you will probably be submitting your manuscript to more than one publisher, you should maintain a record of when and to whom you submitted the manuscript and the responses you receive. All agents do this.

A submission form you can use is shown on page 206.

Manuscript Submission Record

Sent to: _____ _____ _____
               (PUBLISHER)   (ADDRESS)   (ZIP CODE)

Name of Editor: _____Passed on to:_____

Telephone number: _____ FAX Number: _____

Date sent:_____ Follow-up Date: _____

Response: _____

Additional Information: _____

_____

_____

_____

Sent to: _____ _____ _____
               (PUBLISHER)   (ADDRESS)   (ZIP CODE)

Name of Editor:_____ Passed on to: _____

Telephone number:_____ FAX Number: _____

Date sent: _____ Follow-up Date: _____

Response: _____

Additional Information: _____

_____

_____

_____

References

■ In preparation for and during writing, I read many books, mostly for background. Where the books were especially useful, I have mentioned them in the text. The difficulty in this swiftly changing field is that many books on the subject of writing and selling books quickly become out of date. The most useful books are marked with an asterisk.

Applebaum, Judith. *How to Get Happily Published*. 4th ed. New York, NY: HarperCollins, 1992.

*Bernard, André, ed. *Rotten Rejections*. Wainscott, NY: Pushcart Press, 1990.

Bowker Lectures on Book Publishing. New Providence, NJ: R. R. Bowker, 1957.

Brown, Renni, and Dave King. *Self Editing for Fiction Writers: How to Edit Yourself into Print*. New York, NY: HarperCollins, 1993.

Bunnin, Brad. *Author Law and Strategies*. Berkeley, CA: Nolo Press, 1983.

Coser, Lewis, A., Charles Kadushin, and Walter W. Powell. *Books: The Culture and Commerce of Publishing*. New York, NY: Basic Books, 1982.

Curtis, Richard. *How To Be Your Own Literary Agent*. Rev. ed. Boston, MA: Houghton Mifflin, 1994.

80 Years of Best Sellers, 1895-1975. New Providence, NJ: R. R. Bowker, 1977.

Evans, Glen, ed. *The Complete Guide to Writing Non-Fiction*. Cincinnati, OH: Writer's Digest, 1983.

*Garvey, Mark, ed. *1995 Writer's Market*. Cincinnati, OH: Writer's Digest Books, 1994.

*Gross, Gerald. *Editors on Editing*. 3rd ed. New York, NY: Grove Press, 1993.

*Herman, Jeff. *Insider's Guide to Book Editors, Publishers, and Literary Agents*. 1995-1996 ed. Rocklin, CA: Prima Publishing, 1995.

Hoover's Guide to the Book Business. Austin, TX: Reference Press, 1993.

*Kaplan, Dorlene V., and Lawrence H. Caplan. *Guide to Writers Conferences*, 4th ed. Coral Gables, FL: Shaw Guides, 1992.

Larsen, Michael. *How to Write a Book Proposal*. Cincinnati, OH: Writer's Digest Books, 1985.

Levoy, Gregg. *The Business of Writing*. Cincinnati, OH: Writer's Digest Books, 1992.

Literary Market Place 1995. New Providence, NJ: R. R. Bowker, 1994.

Polking, Kirk, ed. *A Beginner's Guide to Getting Published*. Cincinnati, OH: Writer's Digest Books, 1987.

Steinberg, Saul. *Writing For Your Life*. Wainscott, NY: Pushcart, Press, 1992.

Strickland, Bill. *On Being a Writer*. Cincinnati, OH: Writer's Digest Book, 1992.

Acknowledgments

The author wishes to express his appreciation to the experts who read the manuscript and made very valuable suggestions:

Jerry Gross, the editor of the revised third edition of *Editors on Editing* and a former associate at New American Library. Jerry lectures at writers workshops. His practical suggestions were very valuable.

Marc Jaffe, an experienced and distinguished paperback and hardcover editor. During his long tenure as editor-in-chief at Bantam Books, Marc helped create and edited some of America's most successful authors. Marc now has his own imprint at Houghton Mifflin and lectures at many writers workshops.

Kendra Marcus, a successful agent for children's books who, with great insight, made many valuable suggestions at an early stage and just before the manuscript was submitted.

Gene Winnick and Evan Marshall, two outstanding literary agents familiar with the New York and international publishing scene.

Robert Halper, Esq., Partner with whom I work very closely at Cowan, Liebowitz & Latman, P.C. For the last ten years we have worked on many deals together. He made many valuable suggestions throughout the manuscript.

Baila H. Celedonia, Esq., Partner at Cowan, Liebowitz & Latman, P.C., who brought her special expertise to bear on the copyright areas of the manuscript.

Maureen Sheehan, Esq., Associate at Cowan, Liebowitz & Latman, P.C., who now handles most of our active practice in author-publisher contracts.

Della van Heyst, Director of the Stanford Professional Course, who has been generous in allowing me to teach at Palo Alto for the last twelve years. She reviewed the manuscript from the point of view of an educator.

Special thanks also go to the following people: Marcia Levin, my wife, who read the manuscript with a sharp pencil many times. She is an author in her own right and her many valuable suggestions and changes allowed my voice to come through;

Susan Santaniello, my assistant, who cleaned up the numerous drafts of my word-processed text with the eye of a professional writer;

And without whom this would never have appeared:

Phil Wood, the most creative publisher in the world today, and an extraordinary group of associates: Kirsty Melville, Jim Donovan, Kimberley Spears, Mariah Bear, and Clancy Drake, who by their editing made this by far a better book than I could ever make it.

About the Author

Rather than ask an editor to look me up in *Who's Who* and describe my background, I prefer to do what I do at the first session of my Publishing Law class at New York Law School and, for that matter, any time I meet a group to talk about books and publishing. I always begin by introducing myself and describing my background in publishing. So, here goes:

My publishing life has been divided into three acts. Act One is the more than sixteen years I spent with Grosset & Dunlap, now a subsidiary of the Putnam Group. Grosset, when I joined the company in 1950 as the lowly Assistant to the Assistant Sales Manager of their new subsidiary, Wonder Books, was a distinguished privately held company founded at the turn of the century and noted for its series books—Nancy Drew, Tom Swift, and books featuring some thirteen other fictional heroes and heroines.

During the high growth years of the fifties and sixties, Grosset and its sister company, Bantam Books, became a leading publisher in mass market children's and paperback books. I moved through the company with increasing responsibility until, in 1960, I became Senior Vice President of the parent company and a member of the Board of Directors. In these sixteen plus years I was involved in every aspect of publishing and participated in the explosive growth of the juvenile, adult fiction, and nonfiction lists, both in hardcover and paperback.

Act Two opened when the Times Mirror Company, in 1966, asked me to become President of their Book Group. Times Mirror was primarily a newspaper publisher, and they were just building their book publishing business. I was asked to oversee such distinguished companies as New American Library, one of the pioneers in mass market paperback publishing; Harry N. Abrams, the most distinguished of all art book publishers in the world; and World Publishing Company, a dictionary, Bible, reference, and juvenile publisher, as well as companies in the fields of law and medicine. I spent the next seventeen years as the head of this major publishing business, helping it achieve a size that put it among the ten largest U.S. publishers.

During this period I was deeply involved as Chairman of New American Library, which published the first paperback books of Stephen King, Robin Cook, Erica Jong, and many others. NAL in its Signet line published over 300 books a year and, while I dealt with the superstars, I was also involved in editorial policy-making affecting the hundreds of other authors who appeared on the NAL list. Also, while head of the Times Mirror book businesses, I was fortunate enough to be elected to Chairman of the American Association of

Publishers, be on the first publishers' mission to China after the cultural revolution, and to be very active in the publishing community.

Act Three began, at sixty-one years of age, when I decided it was time to achieve my lifelong dream: to become a lawyer. While in charge of the Times Mirror Book Group, and with the forbearance of my boss, to whom I shall always be grateful, I enrolled in New York Law School and studied at night for four long years, changing from my three-piece office attire into a Mets jacket and riding the Lexington Avenue subway to school.

When I reached sixty-five, in 1983, I retired from Times Mirror, having graduated from law school in June of that year. I passed the bar examination in February 1984, and was admitted to the practice of law.

For the last eleven years I have been counsel to the distinguished intellectual property firm of Cowan, Liebowitz & Latman in New York. During this period, I have represented authors, negotiated their contracts, lectured at the Stanford University Professional Publishing Course each year, and been generally very very busy. Not being available to serve as a literary agent on a regular basis, I counseled the authors who came to me, such as Harvey Mackay, the author of *How to Swim With the Sharks Without Being Eaten Alive*, on how to sell their own books, negotiating their contracts for them after they found the publisher. It was out of my publishing and legal experience that I developed my "Eight Step Program for Selling Your Book." I tested this program in presentations to writers' groups, composed of mostly unpublished and aspiring authors, and my everyday practice.

I am part of a publishing family. My wife, Marcia, is an author of some twenty-five picture books and seven teenage novels. My older son, Jeremy, wrote two successful novels, and then was lured away by Hollywood as a screenwriter and director. My younger son, Hugh, owns his own art-book publishing house, Hugh Lauter Levin Associates, Inc. My daughter, Wendy Newby, who is Director of a learning disability clinic, is engaged in writing her Ph.D. dissertation.

I hope after reading my book and sharing these experiences with me that you, too, will become part of my "family."

Martin P. Levin

Index

Advances
  for book clubs, 128
  in contract, 143-46
  for hardcover-softcover deals, 130
  income from, 120-21
  for juvenile books, 27
  for mass market, 127-28
  nonrepayment of, 141, 142
  payment of, 105-6, 108
  repayment of, 138-39, 140
  royalties deducted from, 123-24.
    See also Royalties
  warranty and indemnification and, 132
Authors
  feedback to, 40
  negotiations with, 103-11
  right to publisher's assistance, 125-27
  rights to be granted to, 113-20
  using ideas done/not done before, 8-9
  See also Manuscript; Writing
Authors Guild, The, 135, 146, 154-55,
    161-62

Book clubs, 128, 147-48
Book proposal(s), 45-52
  bio for, 49-50, 87-89
  components of, 53-54
  cover letter for, 48, 53, 58-61, 89
  format of, 45, 46-47, 89-90
  organizing, 50-51, 89-101
  query letter for, 40, 47, 53, 54-58
  sample chapter(s) for, 9-10, 49, 51, 54,
    73-86, 89
  SASEs with, 39, 47
  successful methods for, 12-13, 51, 52
  summary for, 48-49, 54, 62-66, 89
  table of contents for, 49, 54, 67-73, 89
  what not to include in, 50
  See also Manuscript

Contract
  on advances, 120-21, 143-46
    repayment of, 138-39, 140
  on advertising and marketing, 131
  on agreement to publish, 141-43
  on anticipated returns, 124-25
  on arbitration, 133-34, 160
  on author noncompetition, 153
  on author's agent, 157-58
  on author's copies, 156
  on author's property, 156
  on book outline, 126, 136, 154

  on copyright, 150-51
  on electronic rights, 161-62
  on grant of rights. *See* Rights, grant of
  on hardcover-softcover deals, 130
  on imprints, 136-37
  on income, 120-25
  on in/out of print, 133, 155-56
  on lawyers' provisions, 158-60
  on licenses, 157
  on manuscript specifics, 138-40
  negotiating, 103-11, 162-63
  on option, 132-33, 153-55
  on permissions, 138, 157
  on prior rights of approval, 130-31
  on proofs, 140-41, 143
  on public availability, 135
  on related materials, 138, 139
  on reprints, 155, 157
  on reserve for returns, 149-50
  on royalties, 121-22, 124, 143-46
    payments of, 149-50
    statements, 149-50
  on sale to third party, 131
  on satisfactory manuscript, 120-21,
    125-27, 132, 136, 138-39
  standard, 112-34, 135-63
  on subsidiary rights. *See* Subsidiary
    rights
  on termination, 133, 141-42, 143, 155
  on territory, 117-18, 137-38, 153
  on timeliness, 132, 138, 139
    of manuscript delivery, 121
    of publishing, 141, 142
    of returning proofs, 140-41
  on warranty and indemnification, 131-
    32, 141-42, 143, 151-53
Copyright
  in contract, 150-51
  grant of rights, 113-14
  infringement, 141-42, 143, 151, 152-53
  intellectual property and, 104
  notices and registration, 138, 139, 151
  for textbooks, 32
  work for hire and, 32
Criticism
  from editors, 10-11, 51
  from fellow writers, 10, 16
  from self, 7-8, 9, 44, 50-51, 53

Editor(s)
  acquisition, 28

author negotiations with, 103-11
contacting, 15-17, 37, 40
decision-making process, 42
finding right, 14, 24, 26, 46, 191
information on, 11, 22, 24, 26, 29, 42, 46
need for authors, 6, 52, 102
review of submissions, 37-38, 40-41,
    50-51
selection criteria, 41-44

Fiction
literary agents for, 40
manuscripts, 38
responses to submission of, 40
selection criteria, 43
See also Book proposal(s)

Hardcover books, 21, 26, 127, 130

Illustrations, 27, 50, 138, 139
Income
from advances, 120-21
early payment for subsidiary rights,
    129-30
financial analysis of, 104-5, 106-7
method of payment, 123-25
from royalties, 121-22, 124
from subsidiary rights, 122-23

Juvenile books, 27, 30, 31, 32, 50, 147

Lawyers, publishing, 104, 107-8, 113,
    135-63
Libel, 141-42, 143, 151-53
Literary agents
for contract representation, 113
listings, 190
payment to, 157-58
publisher preference for, 103
as self, 1-6
selling techniques, 18-19.
    See also Selling program
Literary Market Place
book trade and professional events, 190
for correct addresses, 192
editors in, 22, 24, 26, 29
    freelance, 10-11
editors-in-chief in, 28
how to use, 22, 179-91, 189
imprints in, 26
lawyers in, 107
literary agents in, 190
publishers in, 12, 13, 17

conglomerates, 182-89
small press, 189
textbook and supplements, 30, 31
trade book, 22
university press, 29
U.S., 180-82
updating, 18
writers conferences and workshops in, 190
yellow pages, 190-91

Magazine articles, 47, 128
Manuscript
finished
    in contract, 138-40
    format of, 138, 139
    satisfactory, 120-21, 125-27, 132, 136,
        138-39
    timely manner of, 121
submission of unsolicited, 11
    acceptance of, 36-37
    complete, 38, 48, 51, 89, 102
    editors' suggestions for, 40-41
    following up on, 14, 51
    multiple, 39
    packaging, 40
    quantity and quality of, 37
    record of, 205-6
    responses to, 38-41
    selling techniques, 164-65.
        See also Selling program
Mass market books, 25-26, 106, 127-28

Nonfiction
competitive books of, 51
manuscripts, 38, 41
organization of material, 44
responses to submission of, 40, 41
selection criteria, 43-44
See also Book proposal(s)

Paperback books, 25-26, 130
Permissions, 51, 138, 139, 157
Professional books, 27-29
Promotion
by publisher, 26, 131
by self, 50, 87
Publishers
best bets for, 17, 192-204
contacting, 15-17
finding best, 13-14, 20-35, 191
imprints, 26, 136-37
lists, 40
marketing, 23, 26, 131

PubSpeak, 168-78
researching, 22-24, 34-35, 40
U.S., 180-82
    conglomerates, 182-89
    See also specific types
Publishers Weekly, 18, 31, 34, 179, 191

Reference books, subscription, 30
Rejections
    form letters for, 38-39
    by successful authors, 4-5
    using, profitably, 14-15
Religious books, 33-34
Right(s)
    of approval, 130-31
    electronic, 123, 161-62
    foreign, 129
    grant of, 113-20, 137-38
        form, 114-16
        language, 116-17
        territory, 117-18, 137-38, 153
        time, 118-20
    in print, 133
    of privacy, 151-53
    publication, 103
    termination, 133
    See also Contract
Royalties
    basis of, 105, 108
    in contract, 143-46
    deducted from advances, 123-24.
        See also Advances
    for electronic rights, 161-62
    for El-Hi textbooks and supplements,
        31, 32
    for hardcover-softcover deals, 130
    income from, 121-22, 124
    for mass market, 127-28
    negotiating, 106-8
    payments of, 149-50
    reduced, 143-46
    reserve for returns, 124-25
    statements, 124, 129-30, 149-50
    withholding of, 152

Scholarly books, 29-30
Self-publishing, 2-3, 165
Selling program (8-step), 12-19
    find the best publisher (2), 13-14
    keep reading (8), 18
    network (6), 15-17
    submit to right editor (3), 14

summary, 18-19
think small (7), 17
use of, by literary agents, 18-19
use patience and persistence (4), 14
use rejection profitably, 14-15
write a winning proposal (1), 12-13
Small presses, 189
Subsidiary rights, 106, 108-9, 127-29
    audio and video, 128-29, 147, 148
    book club, 128, 147-48
    dramatic, 123, 129, 146-47, 148
    early payment for, 129-30
    electronic, 147, 148, 149
    English language, 146, 148
    foreign, 129
    grant of, 146-48
    for hardcover-softcover deals, 130
    income from, 122-23
    magazine, 128
    mass market, 147-48
    merchandising, 129, 147, 148
    method of payment of, 123-25
    microfilm, 146, 148
    movie and television, 129, 146-47, 148
    print, 146
    reprint, 146, 148
    retained, 123, 129, 147
    royalty payments on, 150
    selection, 146, 148
    serial, 146, 148
    share of receipts of, 148-49
    translation, 147, 148

Technology, 31, 32, 34, 123, 161
Textbooks, 30-33
Trade books, 21-24, 106
Trade exhibits/shows
    publisher research at, 23
    specific, 16-17, 23, 31, 190, 192

University press books, 29-30

Writers
    conferences, 10, 15-16, 40, 190
    organizations, 16
    retreats and residences, 16
    workshops, 10, 190
Writing
    as career, 5-6, 165
    for catalogs, 23
    for textbooks and supplements, 30-33
    See also Authors